OUR DIALOGUE WITH ROME

GEORGE B. CAIRD

OUR DIALOGUE
WITH ROME

THE SECOND VATICAN COUNCIL
AND AFTER

The Congregational Lectures
1966

OXFORD UNIVERSITY PRESS
LONDON   OXFORD   NEW YORK
1967

Oxford University Press

LONDON OXFORD NEW YORK
GLASGOW TORONTO MELBOURNE WELLINGTON
CAPE TOWN SALISBURY IBADAN NAIROBI LUSAKA ADDIS ABABA
BOMBAY CALCUTTA MADRAS KARACHI LAHORE DACCA
KUALA LUMPUR HONG KONG TOKYO

First published by Oxford University Press, London, 1967

SET AT THE ALDEN PRESS (OXFORD) LTD.
AND PRINTED IN GREAT BRITAIN
AT THE UNIVERSITY PRESS, OXFORD
BY VIVIAN RIDLER, PRINTER TO THE UNIVERSITY

Preface

=========

I HAVE two reasons for wishing to thank the Congregational Memorial Hall and Library Trust for their invitation to me to give these lectures. I prize highly the honour they have done me in adding my name to the roll of distinguished scholars and churchmen who have delivered the Congregational Lectures in the past. But I am glad also to have been given this opportunity to discharge in some small way my great debt of gratitude to the International Congregational Council for asking me to be one of their observers at the Second Vatican Council, and to the Roman Catholic Church, especially the Secretariat for Promoting Christian Unity, for the invitation to attend the sessions of the Council, and for the unfailing courtesy, hospitality, and friendship with which we were surrounded during our visits to Rome.

These lectures are addressed in the first instance to Congregationalists, and they represent one man's opinion, for which neither the Congregational Church in England and Wales nor the International Congregational Council should be held responsible. But I hope that I may have succeeded in conveying something of the spirit of the Council not only to my own church but to a wider public, and that Roman Catholics, too, may benefit from seeing what the Council has meant to one from a very different tradition who counted it a high privilege to be there.

I am grateful to Professor Albert Outler and Dr. Nathaniel Micklem for permission to use quotations on pp. 5-6 and 7-8, and to Father Walter Abbott, S.J. for permission to use the English translation of the documents of Vatican II of which he was the general editor.

G.B.C.

Oxford, 1967

Contents

1. *The Meaning of Dialogue*

────

Just over a hundred years ago, on 8 December 1864, Pope Pius IX, driven from his early liberalism by the revolutions of 1848 and their stormy sequel, issued an encyclical letter, *Quanta Cura*, which presented an image of the Papacy, not as *defensor fidei*, but as *damnator errorum*. He and his predecessors, he declared,

> had nothing ever more at heart than by their most wise letters and constitutions to unveil and condemn all those heresies and errors which, being adverse to our divine faith, to the doctrine of the Catholic Church, to purity of morals, and to the eternal salvation of men, have frequently excited violent tempests, and have miserably afflicted both Church and State. For which cause the same our Predecessors have, with apostolic fortitude, constantly resisted the nefarious enterprises of wicked men, like raging waves of the sea foaming out their own confusion, and promising liberty whereas they are the slaves of corruption, have striven by their deceptive opinions and most pernicious writings to raze the foundations of the Catholic religion and of civil society, to remove from among men all virtue and justice, to deprave the mind and judgment of all, to turn away from true moral training unwary persons, and especially inexperienced youth, miserably to corrupt such youth, to lead it into the snares of error, and at length tear it from the bosom of the Catholic Church.

Upon that resounding exordium there followed the Syllabus of Errors, which comprehensively condemned all the intellectual movements of a Europe still struggling to emerge into democratic nationhood.

Four years later, when the Pope summoned the Catholic bishops to the first Vatican Council, he wrote a letter to the bishops of the eastern churches inviting them to Rome, not as members of the Council, but to make their submission to his sovereign authority. At the same time he wrote another letter, to Protestants and other non-Catholics, urging them to make the Council an occasion for their repentance and return to the one true fold, since none of the societies to which they belonged exercised any authority from the Lord. They were not invited. As one contemporary commentator put it:

There is in the West no person who has authority, even in name, over others; there are none who stand in the position of the Eastern Bishops, so the Pope, looking over the wild waste of the waters of heresy, saw nobody to whom he could in particular direct his words. He has invited none to Rome, for there is nobody with a pretence to authority among them; but he has most tenderly told them of the perilous course they have taken, and of the certain ruin at the end. (H. Vaughan, *The Year of Preparation for the Vatican Council*, p. 116).

A certain Dr. Cumming of the Church of Scotland wrote first to the Archbishop of Westminster, Henry Edward Manning, and subsequently to the Pope to ask whether there would be an opportunity for those who dissented from the Roman Catholic Church to put forward the reasons they had for doing so, and received the reply that the Church, being infallible in matters relating to faith and morals, 'cannot permit errors which it has carefully considered, judged, and condemned, to be again brought under discussion.' And in this mood the Council proceeded to declare the dogma of Papal infallibility.

It is not to be supposed, however, that this decision silenced the Protestants, or that they were any more irenical in their utterances, though equally convinced that they spoke from a sober charity. In the *Contemporary Review* for October 1874, for example, William Ewart Gladstone, recently relieved of the onerous duties of the premiership, wrote an article describing the present period of Catholic history, 'when Rome has substituted for the proud boast of *semper eadem* a policy of violence and change in faith, when she has refurbished, and paraded anew, every rusty tool she was fondly thought to have disused; when no one can become her convert without renouncing his moral and mental freedom, and placing his civil loyalty and duty at the mercy of another; and when she has equally repudiated modern thought and ancient history'. Later in the same year Gladstone was to claim that, had he been addressing himself to Roman Catholics and not to his own constituency, he would no doubt have used more temperate language; but by that time the cat was out of the bag.

The Syllabus of Errors and the Decrees of the First Vatican Council dictated the attitude of the Roman Church to other Christians for nearly a century, during which most other Christians continued to respond with the defensive suspicions of Gladstone. To be sure, there were all along many instances of individual cordiality and understanding; but the official position remained unchanged, even when the Ecumenical Movement reached its climax in the formation of the World Council of Churches. The change came only when Pope John XXIII, having convoked the Second Vatican Council, established the Secretariat for Promoting Christian Unity under the benign leadership of Cardinal Bea, invited all other Christian communions to send official observers to the Council, and arranged that the observers should be given preferential treatment at every point. Only when we compare the documents of the Second Vatican Council with those of the First, do we begin to recognize the full magnitude of the change. It was Pope John who enabled the Church of Rome to make a clean break with the suspicions and denunciations of a bitter past, and to invite others to make a similar break and join them in a new beginning. But it remained for his successor to put his achievement into eloquent and moving words. It was Pope Paul VI who first addressed the observers as 'beloved brothers in Jesus Christ', who publicly asked pardon from God and his brother Christians for any blame incurred by Rome in the divisions of the church, who spoke of 'the true religious patrimony we share in common, which has been preserved and in part even well developed among our separated brethren'. (Opening address to the Second Session of the Council, 29 September 1963). Above all, it was he who made the word 'dialogue' almost the catchword of the Council.

The change was received by different churches and their observers with different degrees of cordiality. My friend Professor Albert Outler, in a speech which he made at a reception given by the Paulist Fathers in honour of the observers and the American hierarchy, declared that, as there were four parties among the Roman Catholics at the Council (diehards, conservatives, progressives, and arsonists), so there were four types of observer: Hussite, sceptic, admirer, and visionary.

The Hussites believe that there is still time for you to revoke our safe-conduct passes and to close the Council with an auto-da-fé in the Piazza di Sant' Uffizio. The sceptics see many outward signs of change but, knowing Rome of old, they regard these as illusions. The admirers readily admit that great things have been wrought here in the Council, but they fear that once the tumult and shouting are over, the tide of reform will ebb away, leaving only your noise-makers clamouring for what might have been. The visionaries, however, believe that you really have let the ecumenical genie out of the bottle, that you have opened Pandora's box of trouble and hope.

When we were first told that, instead of being called to renounce our errors and return to the bosom of Mother Church, we were being invited to dialogue, there were some from the East as well as from the Protestant West—Outler's Hussites and sceptics—who regarded the change as superficial and even insidious. There was, they assured us, no substantial change of heart. Having failed to win us by threats and violence, Rome was now trying to seduce us by kindness. She was not yet prepared for give and take. No doubt there were Catholics also who hoped that this was true. And it could not be denied that the *schema De Ecclesia* reaffirmed the primacy of the Pope, and even the *schema De Oecumenismo* asserted that only the Catholic Church possessed the totality of revealed truth and all the means of grace. According to this view, all that dialogue could mean was that Catholic theologians would attempt to restate the unchanging truth of Catholic doctrine in such a way as to remove any unnecessary cause of offence and misunderstanding; and the Roman Church was still naively expecting that, once this was done, light would inevitably dawn on souls separated only by an unfortunate accident of history from their true home.

In a moment I shall give you reasons for regarding this as a niggardly estimate of dialogue. But even if this had been all that was intended, I should still have four reasons for maintaining that it would have been a great advance.

(1) One of the most deplorable facts about even the bloodless

wars of religion in the past has been the repeated breach of the
ninth commandment. Too often Protestants and Catholics
alike have been content to score shabby victories by demolish-
ing a mere caricature of the others' position. Real and important
differences have been obscured by a welter of sheer and often
unscrupulous fiction. Accordingly, the Decree on Ecumenism
calls for 'every effort to eliminate words, judgments, and actions
which do not respond to the condition of separated brethren
with truth and fairness' (par. 4). To this end the Decree on
Priestly Formation lays down that training for the priesthood
should include studies leading 'to a more adequate understanding of the churches and ecclesial communities separated
from the Roman Apostolic See' (par. 16).

(2) It is also laid down in the Decree on Ecumenism that 'the
manner and order in which Catholic belief is expressed
should in no way become an obstacle to dialogue with our
brethren' (par. 11); and this was a principle systematically
observed in the debates in St. Peter's. The withdrawal of the
schema on the two sources of revelation and the substitution of
a new document in which Scripture and tradition are together
said to constitute a single source was clearly influenced by this
consideration. After being for many years a member of the
World Council of Churches' commission on 'Tradition and
the Traditions', it was interesting for me to observe that Rome
seemed to be depreciating the significance of tradition precisely
at the moment when we Protestants were discovering that we
after all had a tradition of our own. The inclusion of the whole
schema on the Blessed Virgin as Chapter VIII of the Dogmatic
Constitution on the Church is another example of the same
process at work; for though Mary is there entitled Mediatrix
(par. 62), it is explicitly stated that this is not to be understood

in such a way as to 'take away from or add anything to the dignity and efficacy of Christ the one Mediator'. The chapter, moreover, contains a strong warning to theologians and preachers: 'Let them painstakingly guard against any word or deed which could lead separated brethren or anyone else into error regarding the true doctrine of the Church' (par. 67). The Grand Master of the Order of Preachers (Dominicans) asked that this warning be deleted, since it implied that theologians and preachers had been in the habit of misrepresenting the Catholic faith by exaggeration; but the Council Fathers voted overwhelmingly in favour of keeping it.

(3) The Council clearly recognized that, though divine truth may be unchanging, the forms in which it is expressed will necessarily vary from age to age. This, as we shall see later, was one of the most important points made by Pope John XXIII in the address with which he opened the first session of the Council. It is also forcefully stated in the very impressive Decree on Priestly Formation, which encourages an historical approach to the Bible, and to Church history, to doctrine, and to philosophy, combined with a sound grasp of that which is 'perennially valid'. This opens up the possibility that, on some points at least, Catholics and Protestants might find that they are, after all, at one in the area of the perennially valid, however much they might be at variance in the forms of expression. Among ourselves there has been no more persistent and eloquent advocate of this thesis than Nathaniel Micklem, and I was delighted to find the following characteristic utterance in his latest book, *My Cherry Tree*.

I will begin with the gigantic paradox that I, who am an unrepenting (though dissatisfied) Protestant, believe the doctrine of transubstantiation, and the majority of Roman Catholics do not. I begin with the second and easier part of this at first sight ridiculous affirmation. I affirm that most Roman Catholics do not believe this dogma because it is a highly philosophical theory which they are quite incapable of understanding and I am prepared to affirm that I believe it, because if one can by an exercise of historic imagination bring oneself to think in the old terms of substance and accident, which the dogma presupposes, then I think the matter must be put as this dogma puts it. . . . Why does the Roman Catholic believe, or think he believes, the doctrine of transubstantiation? Because (to put it very briefly) when the bell rings at Mass, he is aware of the veritable presence of Christ and worships him. What Christian can deny this awful and profound experience?

To this let me add another example, which you may consider even more paradoxical. Of all the differences between us, I suppose the one most frequently treated as a source of contention is Papal infallibility. I do not doubt that in the past this dogma has been expounded in terms which made it totally unacceptable to Protestants. But, as it is treated in the documents of Vatican II, and especially in Chapter III of *De Ecclesia*, it seems to me designed to safeguard two beliefs to which any Congregationalist would gladly give his assent: the permanent and full sufficiency of the historic deposit of faith, the revelation of God in Jesus Christ; and the confidence that the Holy Spirit will at all times lead the Church into all truth. Whatever qualms we may still have about the form of expression, we should be ready to recognize and give full credit to the intention behind it.

(4) One of the most important results of the Council was the discovery by the bishops of the real differences among themselves. They came from the ends of the earth to meet as strangers, united in the confidence that they belonged to a monolithic church. But as the first personal strangeness wore

off, they found that they were in a deeper sense strangers to one another's mentality. Many of them have openly confessed that the process by which they were brought to a common mind on the weighty matters of the Council's agenda was for them a painful discipline, in which all their most cherished beliefs and prejudices were exposed to a penetrating scrutiny. Even the common use of Latin in the debates in St. Peter's served as often as not to emphasize the cultural diversity of the speakers. As has sometimes been said of the British and Americans, they found themselves divided by a common language. This experience helped to bring home to them a truth which on more than one occasion I heard put into words, that Rome had too long confused unity with uniformity, and must work towards a far more catholic comprehensiveness, which would leave room for plenty of regional variety, as well as for differences of emphasis within a single locality. This means that our ultimate union with Rome need not be conceived in terms of submission or even of compromise. All this seems to me to show that a genuine and worthwhile dialogue could be conducted between Catholics and Protestants without either side being compelled to relinquish any of their deepest convictions.

When all this has been said, however, I must repeat that this is only a small part of what is intended by dialogue. My immediate reasons for saying this are to be found in two of the earliest addresses of Pope Paul after his accession to the Chair of St. Peter: the allocution with which he opened the second session of the Council, and his greeting to the observers at an audience held three weeks later in his private library. On both these occasions the Pope deliberately drew attention to the possible misinterpretation of his church's new ecumenical friendliness, and begged the observers and the churches they represented to lay aside their suspicions. 'We lay no snares; we are not motivated by temporal interest. We owe our faith, which we believe to be divine, the most candid and firm attachment. But at the same time we are convinced that this does not constitute an obstacle to the desired understanding with our separated brethren, precisely because it is the truth of the Lord and therefore the principle of union and not of distinction or separation. At any rate we do not wish to make of our faith an occasion for polemics.' 'Our attitude conceals no trap; nor does it succumb to any intention of minimizing the difficulties in the way of a complete and definitive understanding; it does not shrink from the delicate nature of the discussion nor from the pain of hope deferred.' At the audience he went out of his way to emphasize the reciprocal nature of the encounter. 'Approaching, meeting, greeting, becoming acquainted, conversing—what could be more simple, more natural, more human? Yes, indeed! But here there is something more: listening to one another; praying for one another; and, after such long years of separation, after such grievous contention, beginning to love one another: this is what makes this meeting memorable and full of promise.' The audience itself bore out his words; for he agreed that Professor Skydsgaard should first address him on behalf of the observers, acknowledged the most telling points of the professor's speech with a typical gesture of appreciation, and then picked up and developed these and other points in his own reply.

But perhaps the most encouraging fact was that on neither of these two occasions did the Pope try to disguise the vast outstanding differences between us, which must be faced with honesty and candour. 'We are aware', he said in his opening allocution, 'that serious and complicated questions remain to be studied, treated and resolved. We would wish that this could be done immediately on account of the love of Christ that urges us on. But we also realize that these problems require many conditions before satisfactory solutions can be reached, conditions which are as yet premature. Hence we are not afraid to await patiently the blessed hour of perfect reconciliation.' And again at the audience: 'The esteem in which we hold yourselves and the institutions and Christian values you represent makes easy for us the task of embarking with you on the great dialogue, even though no one today, granted the doctrinal divergences that remain unresolved, can predict how long it will last.'

From all this it should be clear that, when Rome speaks of dialogue, she envisages a process in which she is as ready to listen and learn as to expound and teach. But how is it possible for a church which still regards herself as the only authorized repository of divine truth to learn from others? The simple, pragmatic answer to this would be that the dialogue has unofficially been going on for many years; Roman theologians, and particularly Roman biblical scholars, have read the books of Protestant scholars, have entered into discussion with them, have been influenced by their ideas. The proof of this is plainly to be seen on almost every page of the Council documents, but I must limit myself to a handful of examples. The Declaration on Religious Liberty defines faith as man's free response to God: 'the act of faith is of its very nature a free act' (par. 9). In the Dogmatic Constitution on the Church and frequently elsewhere it is said that all Christians without distinction are called to the life of holiness and perfection. The same document reminds bishops that 'those ministers who are endowed with sacred power are servants of their brethren' (par. 18); and the

Decree on the Bishops' Pastoral Office in the Church puts more emphasis on their duties and responsibilities than on their rights and authority. (I shall have more to say on this subject in my third lecture on the nature of authority.) The Decree on the Apostolate of the Laity speaks of the need to develop in all members of the church a Christian judgement and a Christian conscience; and this decree, together with Chapters IV and V of *De Ecclesia*, represents, as many of the bishops themselves pointed out, the first serious pronouncement the Roman Church has ever made about the distinctive part the laity must play in the work and mission of the church. The Decree on the Missionary Activity of the Church argues from the assumption that 'particular churches are bound to mirror the universal church as perfectly as possible.' (Par. 20; cf. Const. on the Church, par. 26). And throughout all the documents there is an emphasis on the Holy Spirit long absent from Roman Catholic teaching. Above all, as I shall show at greater length in the second of these lectures, there is a new attention to Scripture. The Decree on the Appropriate Renewal of the Religious Life urges on the members of religious communities 'a continuous return to the sources of all Christian life' (par. 2), among which the daily reading of Scripture is placed first. The Decree on Priestly Formation declares that 'the study of sacred Scripture . . . ought to be the soul of all theology' (par. 16). And the Dogmatic Constitution on Divine Revelation (par. 12) lays it down that the meaning of Scripture is the meaning intended by the human author, under the guidance of God, and that Scripture must be studied with due regard to its literary forms. I am not suggesting that all these ideas are wholly new to Roman Catholic thought. The new approach to Scripture, for example, was already adumbrated in 1943 in the Papal encyclical *Divino Afflante Spiritu*. But this does not affect my point that in these and many other instances it is possible to detect the influence of a past dialogue with Protestantism.

At this point I must insert a second *caveat*. I have argued that it would be wrong to think of dialogue as Rome's way of imposing by kindness a dogmatic and ecclesiastical authority she has failed to impose by sterner methods. It would be equally superficial to regard dialogue as Rome's way of belatedly catching up with the Protestant Reformation. The truth is, I believe, much more complex and much more exciting; and I propose to explore it now under three heads.

1. *The Development of Doctrine*

It is generally agreed that the Council, for better for worse, has espoused Newman's concept of the development of doctrine. Indeed, it was frequently remarked that, while the First Vatican Council belonged to Manning, the Second belonged to Newman. Newman, as you will remember, just before he changed his allegiance from the Church of England to the Church of Rome, wrote a massive work in which he argued that any idea which is a living force in the life and thought of men must be subject to development, and tried to define the limits within which a developing idea could be said to have retained its identity. The book at that time met with no cordial response in Rome, though he was generously allowed to publish it on the grounds that he had written it before he accepted the Roman obedience. The clearest reference to the development of doctrine in the documents of Vatican II occurs in the Dogmatic Constitution on Divine Revelation.

This tradition which comes from the apostles develops in the Church

with the help of the Holy Spirit. For there is a growth in the understanding of the realities and the words which have been handed
down. . . . For, as the centuries succeed one another, the Church
constantly moves forward toward the fulness of divine truth until
the words of God reach their complete fulfilment in her (par. 8).

But since holy Scripture must be read and interpreted according to
the same Spirit by whom it was written, no less serious attention
must be given to the content and unity of the whole of Scripture, if
the meaning of the sacred texts is to be correctly brought to light.
The living tradition of the whole Church must be taken into
account along with the harmony which exists between elements
of the faith. It is the task of exegetes to work according to these
rules towards a better understanding and explanation of the meaning
of sacred Scripture, so that through preparatory study the judgment
of the Church may mature (par. 12).

No other passage carries us so quickly to the heart of what the
Council has wanted to say about revelation. Scripture and
tradition are not two independent sources of divine truth, but
one. The complete and final revelation of God has been given
in Jesus Christ, and the record of his coming and of the preparation for it is contained in the scriptures of the Old and New
Testaments. To this, tradition adds nothing new. It is rather
the running commentary of the Church's life and thought on
the faith once for all delivered to the saints. Tradition is no
dead system of dogma, but a living process, precisely the process
whereby Scripture comes alive and active in the understanding
and obedience of the church. The Holy Spirit, who is the
source of Scripture, is also its expositor, not simply as a sort of
heavenly commentator, but by supplying the power to make
Scripture the very stuff and substance of the church's existence.
And the process is never finished. 'The Lord has more light
and truth yet to break forth out of his Holy Word.'

The Council itself has been an admirable illustration of this thesis. Those of us who had the privilege of being there could watch the rapid maturing of the Church's judgement on matters both of faith and of conduct. The initial drafts of almost every document were either rejected or totally rewritten, not because they were incompetent summaries of the Church's existing opinion, but because that opinion clearly developed to new positions in the course of public and private debates. Hundreds of speeches made in St. Peter's and thousands of amendments handed in in writing were scrutinized by experts and considered by commissions, and throughout this long, cumbrous procedure the Council somehow never lost momentum. The decisions taken on *De Ecclesia* had immediate repercussions on subsequent documents presented to the Council for debate, and some of these later documents showed further and important advances in the thinking of the Church, beyond the point reached in that central and formative document. Though the two documents I am about to mention are not strictly doctrinal, the simplest way of seeing how the progress of the Council affected the thinking of its participants is to compare one of its earliest products—the slight, arid, and totally inadequate Decree on the Instruments of Social Communication—with one of its latest—the massive, humane, and exciting Pastoral Constitution on the Church in the Modern World.

We observers were constantly led to suppose that our very presence in St. Peter's facilitated this maturing of the Church's judgement. It is true that we had no voice in the debates; but then, neither did the Roman Catholic theologians. Yet, as one speaker after another indicated, our presence was a reminder that these proceedings, nominally *sub secreto*, were in fact taking place before the eyes and ears of an expectant though critical world. Moreover, behind the scenes ample opportunities were provided, both in formal meetings with the Secretariat and in informal contacts in the coffee bars and elsewhere, for us to make our views known. We were there not simply as onlookers, but, in the Pope's own words, as 'the beginning of the great dialogue', which was to be one of the forms of that preparatory study essential to the full maturing of the Church's judgement.

Earlier in this lecture I quoted some words of Pope Paul, from his opening address to the second session of the Council, when he spoke of 'the true religious patrimony we share in common, which has been preserved and in part even well developed among our separated brethren'. I return to these words in order to draw your attention to the phrase 'well developed'. Behind this expression there lie two important assumptions. The first is that even Scripture and the revelation it contains remain a dead word from the past unless they become the word by which men live, unless they enter into the living thought and experience of a Christian community. No part of a religious heritage can be said to be well developed until it has become a stimulus to contemporary thought, conduct, or devotion. We are thus being credited, you see, with what we have so often repudiated—a tradition which we may regard as a revelation from God, and which Rome is at least prepared to consider acknowledging as her own. The second assumption is that in no community, not even in Rome, are all the riches of the apostolic faith equally well developed. Parts of our common religious patrimony which have been well developed in Rome have been neglected by Protestants, and parts which have been well developed among Protestants have received less attention in Rome.

At first blush this might appear to be a flat contradiction of the long-standing claim of Rome to be the one lawful custodian of catholic truth; but the Council Fathers clearly have not felt the two points of view to be incompatible. They have felt free to give full and generous recognition to the cumulative evidence of God's activity outside the boundaries of Roman jurisdiction, yet without abandoning their claim to hold a legal mandate which is unique. To be sure, the Council has been the occasion for a most thoroughgoing revolt against legalism. One document after another was criticized for being too juridical, when it ought to have been pastoral, spiritual, Christocentric. A very interesting example of this revolt was provided by the discussion on the collegial authority of bishops. Vatican I proclaimed that 'the Pope of Rome, when he speaks *ex cathedra*, . . . wields that infallibility with which the Divine Redeemer wished his church to be equipped for the definition of doctrine concerning faith and morals.' Vatican II has said that 'the infallibility promised to the Church resides also in the body of bishops when that body exercises supreme teaching authority with the successor of Peter.' (Const. on the Church, par. 25). The conservatives objected: 'But now we have two independent centres of plenary authority, and this is nonsense.' The answer was: 'This may be nonsense if you are thinking juridically, but not if you are thinking spiritually.' If you believe that the Church is constituted by the presence of Christ and guided by the Holy Spirit, you have every right to assume that the Spirit will bring Pope and bishops to a common mind. Certainly this is how the Pope himself thinks of his own authority in relation to that of the bishops, as may be seen from his encyclical letter *Ecclesiam Suam*. 'In this letter,' he wrote, 'I have deliberately abstained from offering my own opinion in any way on those doctrinal matters with regard to the Church which have been submitted to the judgment of the Ecumenical Council over which I preside. For the present my intention is that an assembly of such weight and authority as this should enjoy full liberty of investigation and discussion. In keeping with the apostolic office of teacher and pastor which I hold as head of the Church, I shall disclose my mind at the proper time and in the proper fashion; and then I shall have no greater wish than this, that my opinion may be clearly in agreement with that of the Council Fathers.'

This new emphasis on spiritual realities helps to explain the new openness of Rome to other churches and her appreciative interest in their traditions. As long as you emphasize the rights and authority of the one true church, it is hard to find a place in your thinking for those who do not acknowledge those rights or accept that authority. But when you give a central place to the presence of Christ and the activity of the Holy Spirit, then you may begin to detect that presence and that activity in quarters where you had not expected to find them. Once a Catholic has begun to discover the activity of God outside the sacramental discipline of his own Church, there is no limit to the territory in which God may be found. Take for example this quotation from the Pastoral Constitution on the Church in the Modern World. 'The People of God believes that it is led by the Spirit of the Lord, who fills the earth. Motivated by this faith, it labours to decipher authentic signs of God's presence and purpose in the happenings, needs, and desires in which this People has a part along with other men of our age' (par. 11). How far we have come from the Syllabus of Errors, when the Church is prepared to detect God's presence in the intellectual, political, and cultural movements of our day! A church which believes itself to be so led by the Spirit of God that it can respond to the prompting of that Spirit wherever he may be at work is surely a church with which we can and ought to be in dialogue. But this healthy revolt against legalism does not mean that the Church of Rome has abandoned its belief in historic transmission. The tension between authority historically transmitted and authority received directly from above is as old as the history of religion. We have been prone to resolve it by ignoring the one and exalting the other. If we are to enter into dialogue with Rome, this is one area in which we must be prepared to think again; and it will be the theme of my third lecture.

2. Continual Reformation of the Church

One of the most startling passages in the whole record of Vatican II occurs in the second chapter of the Decree on Ecumenism. 'Christ summons the Church, as she goes her pilgrim way, to that continual reformation of which she always has need, insofar as she is an institution of men here on earth. Therefore, if the influence of events or of the times has led to deficiencies in conduct, in church discipline, or even in the formulation of doctrine (which must be carefully distinguished from the deposit itself of faith), these should be appropriately rectified at the proper moment' (par. 6). It will help to illustrate what I have just been saying to you about the development of doctrine during the Council, if I attempt to trace for you the stages by which the Council Fathers were led to accept such a remarkable qualification of their former doctrine of the Church's infallibility.

When Pope John summoned the Council, the intention of

it was summed up in the word *aggiornamento*, the emergence of the Church from its mediaeval cocoon into the free and full vitality demanded by the conditions of modern life. This intention is echoed in more than one of the Council documents. The Decree on the Appropriate Renewal of the Religious Life defines renewal as 'two simultaneous processes: a continuous return to the sources of all Christian life . . . and an adjustment of the community to the changed conditions of the times' (par. 2). The whole first part of the Pastoral Constitution on the Church in the Modern World is devoted to an analysis of those changed conditions with which the Church must come to grips. In his opening address to the Council Pope John indicated that he expected this adjustment to extend to doctrine as well as to practical and pastoral concerns. 'The deposit of faith is one thing: the way it is presented is another. For the truths preserved in our sacred doctrine can retain the same substance and meaning under different forms of expression.' But there was so far no suggestion that existing forms of expression might actually be wrong, only that they were ill-adapted to the needs of the present.

A new stage was reached a year later in the opening address of Pope Paul, to which I have already more than once alluded. Now the aims of the Council were said to be not one but four: a new awareness by the Church of its own nature; its reform; the bringing together of all Christians in unity; the dialogue of the Church with the contemporary world. *Aggiornamento*, at least as it was commonly understood, had already slipped into fourth place, and this was because 'it is only after this work of internal sanctification has been accomplished that the Church will be able to show herself to the whole world.' About the need for reform the Pope had this to say:

The Council aims at renewal. Note well, however, that in saying and desiring that, we do not imply that the Catholic Church of today can be accused of substantial infidelity to the mind of her divine Founder. Rather it is the deeper realization of her substantial faithfulness that fills her with gratitude and humility and inspires her with the courage to correct those imperfections which are proper to human weakness. The reform at which the Council aims is not, therefore, a turning upside down of the Church's present way of life or a breaking with what is essential and worthy of veneration in her tradition, but it is rather an honouring of tradition by stripping it of what is unworthy or defective so that it may be rendered firm and faithful.

Notwithstanding the entirely proper qualifications with which this statement was hedged, here was the first authoritative admission that the Church's tradition has a human and fallible side to it, that not all of it is essential and worthy of veneration, and that it cannot in its entirety be regarded as the undiluted revelation of God.

During the weeks that immediately followed this address the Council was engaged in discussion of the vital *schema De Ecclesia*, which at this stage contained no suggestion that the Church might be in constant need of reformation. Nor did the bishops at once take up the Pope's lead on this subject. One or two speeches demanded a more dynamic view of the church which would make it clear that perfection lay ahead in the eschatological future. An Italian bishop declared that the debate proved all the Council Fathers to belong to the *ecclesia quaerens*, and proposed that they should continue their search, since he could see no sign of light breaking in at the present. One of the most outspoken figures of the Council accused laity, clergy, and hierarchy of all being beset by the pastoral heresy of individualism. And in speaking of the laity one of the more colourful cardinals asked the Council to be realistic and remember that they were dealing 'with individuals living in the world and subject to all the laws and weaknesses of human nature'. But I do not recall anyone at this stage making a similar remark about bishops.

The Theological Commission, which, under the chairmanship of Cardinal Ottaviani, had produced this *schema* and was responsible for rewriting it in the light of all the comments received from the Council Fathers, was not generally held to be the most radical of the Council's committees. It is the more remarkable, then, that, when the revised and greatly enlarged document was presented to the Council the following year for voting, it contained this sentence: 'While Christ, "holy, innocent, undefiled", knew nothing of sin, but came to expiate only the sins of the people, the Church, embracing sinners in her bosom, is at the same time holy and always in need of being purified, and incessantly pursues the path of penance and renewal'; and this sentence went unaltered into the final text (par. 8). Rome had, of course, always paid full heed to the sinfulness of her children, providing them with an elaborate penitential system; but here was a conciliar document at last affirming that Mother Church might herself have need of repentance. At the same time, i.e. at the beginning of the third session, the *schema* on Ecumenism appeared in a new draft, which already contained the words I quoted a moment ago from the final text of the decree, together with a footnote indicating that the words 'continual reformation of which the Church always has need, insofar as she is an institution of men here on earth' were taken verbatim from an address delivered a year previously in Italian by the Pope to the Roman Curia. The plain inference is that, if judgement is to begin in the household of God, it must begin at the top. And it is equally plain that in the maturing and ultimate acceptance of this idea the two Popes have given a firm lead to the Church.

Let it once be admitted that the church is in constant need of reform in conduct, discipline, and doctrine, and the implications for ecumenical dialogue are obvious. If the churches should ever be wholly reformed according to the Word of God, they would *ipso facto* find themselves to be one Church. The road to unity lies by way of a more rigorous reformation than any of us has yet been willing to contemplate. The purpose of dialogue, then, is not that two churches should confront each other with their separate traditions and endeavour by bargaining, compromise, and patchwork to reduce the two to one, but that together they should be able to achieve a more thoroughgoing and profitable reformation than either of them could achieve in isolation. The goal of ecumenism is unity, but such unity as can be attained only by a common obedience to the judging, cleansing, and restoring Word of God.

Since the Council ended, some dissatisfaction has been expressed that it has failed to bring about the sweeping changes that *aggiornamento* had seemed to portend. But this is to miss the point. The Council has recognized the limitations of Councils. It has recognized that reform cannot be completed once and for all, let alone be laid on from above by legislation. Legislation may, indeed, provide the indispensable conditions for reform. But genuine reform must come from the roots of the Church, must become a normal part of its day-to-day existence, as the Church constantly finds pardon and renewal in the sources of its faith. Whether that intention is to be implemented and sustained in the Roman Catholic Church may well depend on the willingness of the separated brethren to accept the invitation to dialogue.

3. The Pilgrim People of God

At this point in our argument the objection might well be raised that dialogue seems to be so important to the life of the Church, both for the development of its doctrine and for the maintenance of constant reform, that it would be a tragedy if the achievement of unity should leave the one Church with nobody outside to talk to. Let me make it quite clear that I do not regard this objection as captious or frivolous, even if at the moment it may appear somewhat premature; it raises very serious questions about the nature of the unity we seek. But it assumes, of course, that dialogue must necessarily be with Christians of a different ecclesiastical allegiance. This was certainly the context in which the word first claimed our attention. But as time went by we began to hear of two other forms of dialogue: the interior dialogue of the Church, and the Church's dialogue with the non-Christian world, those of other religions or none. Each of these dialogues arises directly out of the nature of the Church as the pilgrim people of God.

Of all the decisions taken in Vatican II none, I fancy, will prove more far-reaching than the decision to give Chapter II of De Ecclesia the title De Populo Dei—the People of God. Roman Catholics had long been accustomed to give special preference to another designation of the Church, the Mystical Body of Christ, and there were many in the Council who asked for the retention of this as the title for the second chapter of the schema. Now we are all familiar with the Pauline description of the Church as the body of Christ, and we all sing hymns which imply that the Church is in some sense a heavenly reality, since it is constituted by the presence of the risen and exalted Christ. The choice before the Council was therefore admittedly only one of emphasis. But it was still a choice which could have made a world of difference. For to call the Church the mystical body of Christ is to concentrate attention on her heavenly, perfect, and static aspect; whereas to call her the people of God is to concentrate attention on her human, historic, and dynamic character. It is to conjure up a picture of a pilgrim church, moving through the vicissitudes of history, from Abraham to Christ and from Christ into the hope of the future, with all her faults and all her aspirations, living under the judgement of God and by his unfailing mercy, looking always to a destiny as yet unfulfilled. More than this, the destiny of the people of God is larger than her own holiness and perfection, though this is included in it. The Church exists in the world and for the world, and her calling is nothing less than to bring the whole world under the sovereignty of her God. To this end there must clearly be a dialogue with the world. But there must also be an interior dialogue within the Church, in which those who know most about the world pool their experience with those who know most about God.

In the fourth chapter of the Dogmatic Constitution on the Church this dialogue is described in some detail, as it is expected to exist at the parish level. 'An individual layman, by reason of the knowledge, competence, or outstanding ability which he may enjoy is permitted and sometimes even obliged to express his opinion on things which concern the good of the Church.' There follows a detailed treatment of the mutual responsibilities of pastor and laity, leading to this impressive conclusion. 'A great many benefits are to be hoped for from this familiar dialogue between the laity and their pastors: in the laity, a strengthened sense of personal responsibility, a renewed enthusiasm, a more ready application of their talents to the projects of their pastors. The latter, for their part, aided by the experience of the laity, can more clearly and more suitably come to decisions regarding spiritual and temporal matters. In this way, the whole church, strengthened by each one of its members, can more effectively fulfil its mission for the life of the world' (par. 37).

This picture of corporate responsibility, which bears some resemblance to what Congregationalists have always expected, but have not always found, in the Church Meeting, is to have its counterpart in the wider life of the Church. In the diocese there is to be a parallel dialogue between the bishop and his family of priests, he contributing his knowledge of the Church at large, they their intimate experience of the pastoral needs of particular men and women. The bishop 'should exercise the greatest care on behalf of the continual formation of his priests. He should gladly listen to them, indeed, consult them, and have discussions with them about those matters which concern the necessities of pastoral work and the welfare of the diocese. In order to put these ideals into effect, a group or senate of priests representing the presbytery should be established.' (Dec. on the Ministry and Life of Priests, par. 7). This senate of priests is reminiscent also of the more widely publicized synod of bishops, which is to give practical expression to the newly-defined collegial character of the episcopate. For this synod, though it will have legislative powers, will be primarily a consultative body. Its meetings will be an occasion for dialogue, in which Pope and bishops will share their ideas and their problems, and the bishops will put their first-hand knowledge of the regions they represent at the disposal

of the Pope, to enable him the better to fulfil his universal
pastorate.

It should be unnecessary to ask whether the dialogue between
Rome and those whom she calls the separated brethren should
be considered part of the interior dialogue of the Church or
part of the Church's dialogue with the world outside. The
documents of Vatican II leave no doubt that Rome now thinks
of us as brothers in Christ, is ready to accord the name of
church to the societies to which we belong (in the case of the
Congregational Church she did so even before we were
ready to claim it), and recognizes that these churches are
related to the one, holy, catholic, and apostolic Church in a way
that she finds understandably hard to define.

We have received an invitation, and an invitation deserves
an answer. Are we then prepared to abandon the polemics of
the past and to look with new appreciation at a great tradition
which we have never understood because we saw it always
through the eyes of hostility and suspicion? Are we ready to
dig deep beneath the outward forms of faith and practice to
discover whether after all we are not, at some deeper level,
closer to one another than we had supposed? Do we care
enough for the truth of God to attempt to make our own the
heritage of those whose experience of God's grace is foreign
to ours? Are we sincere enough in our belief in constant
reformation under the Word of God to undergo a more
ruthless self-appraisal than ever before? Do we share God's love
for the world deeply enough to regard as an ally anyone who
shares that love, however strange to us may be his mode of
expressing it? For this, and nothing less than this, is the meaning
of 'the great dialogue'.

2. *The Use of Scripture*

A MAN once said to Mark Twain that the Bible worried him, because there was so much in it that he could not understand; to which Mark Twain replied that what worried him in the Bible was the parts he did understand. In this Mark Twain showed himself a true son of the Reformation. For whatever differences there may have been between Lutherans and Calvinists, between Presbyterians and Independents, all the churches of the Reformation agreed in making three affirmations about the Bible: that it must be put into the hands of the ordinary man in a language he could read; that it contained all he needed for his salvation; and that, whatever was necessary for his salvation, he could understand it without further help from academic or ecclesiastical authority. The words of Erasmus echoed and re-echoed across Europe and down the years:

I would have the weakest woman read the Gospels and Paul's epistles. And I wish that they were translated into all languages, that they may be read and known, not only by the Scotch and Irish, but also by the Turks and Saracens. . . . I would that the husbandman at the plough should sing something from hence; that the weaver at his loom should hum them to the tune of his shuttle; that the traveller might beguile the weariness of his journey by narration of this kind.

The following paragraphs from the Westminster Confession

were taken over verbatim in the Savoy Declaration of 1658, the only change being in the distribution of capital letters.

The whole Counsel of God concerning all things necessary for his own Glory, man's Salvation, Faith and Life, is either expresly set down in Scripture, or by good and necessary consequence may be deduced from Scripture; unto which nothing at any time is to be added, whether by new Revelations of the Spirit, or Traditions of men. . . . All things in Scripture are not alike plain in themselves, nor alike clear unto all: yet those things which are necessary to be known, believed, and observed for Salvation, are so clearly propounded and opened in some place of Scripture or other, that not onely the learned, but the unlearned, in a due use of the ordinary means, may attain unto a sufficient understanding of them. (Chap. I, §§ vi, vii)

Over against this the church of the Counter-reformation had pronounced its anathema on anyone who did not accept the authority of the Latin Vulgate, had declared that divine truth was equally to be found in the holy books and in the traditions which had no scriptural basis (*sine scripto traditionibus*), and had insisted that the meaning of Scripture could be determined only by the teaching authority of the Church. Both Protestant and Catholic professed the highest regard for Scripture and were prepared to speak of God as its author. But while the Protestant believed that Scripture must be allowed to speak for itself, and might speak a word by which the Church itself would be judged and compelled to reform its practice or even its doctrine, for the Catholic this was unthinkable, since the true meaning of Scripture could be reached only through the infallible dogmas of the Church. Both Catholic and Protestant made use of Scripture in public and private devotion. But while to the Catholic Scripture and the preached word were a preparation for the grace which could come to him only through the Church's sacramental system, and therefore through the ministrations of the priest, to the Protestant they were the chief of the means of grace, which brought him directly, without priestly meditation, not only to the truth but to the presence of God.

The Protestants, in short, were the People of the Book. No doubt there were other differences between Catholic and Protestant as important as their divergent views of Scripture, but this difference had one momentous corollary. It made it almost impossible for four hundred years for the two sides to enter into fruitful discussion. The Protestant believed that the Word of God must not be bound, and that within the Roman camp it was almost invisible under the weight of its dogmatic shackles; and the Catholic declined to argue with anyone whose heretical severance from the Apostolic See had disqualified him from holding any opinion whatever about a book which he considered to be his Church's private possession. In my first lecture I raised the question whether genuine and profitable dialogue was possible between Rome and those whom she now calls the separated brethren. Clearly no such dialogue could proceed far if it were to come to an impasse whenever the interpretation of Scripture was involved. We must ask therefore whether at this point the Second Vatican Council has marked a significant change.

That the Council documents show a remarkable advance on Rome's earlier attitude to the Bible is obvious to anyone who takes the trouble to read them. There is an altogether new emphasis on the centrality of Scripture. Not only are all the documents full of scriptural references, but Scripture is said to be of paramount importance both for the training of the clergy and for the reform of the liturgy. More attention must be paid to the sermon, and sermons are to be more scriptural. 'The treasures of the Bible are to be opened up more lavishly, so that richer fare may be provided for the faithful at the table of God's Word.' (Decree on the Liturgy, par. 51.) There is a welcome insistence on sound exegesis. Those of us who were in St. Peter's in early October, 1963, were delighted to hear one day Cardinal Bea criticizing the *schema De Ecclesia* because the scriptural passages it cited did not mean what the authors of that *schema* wanted them to mean, and the next day Cardinal Ruffini, from the opposite end of the ecclesiastical spectrum, scolding the commission for twisting other texts in support of their doctrine of episcopal collegiality. Quotations from the New Testament are often explicitly said to be from the Greek text, because the Vulgate at that point is inferior, seminaries are urged to provide instruction in the biblical languages, and there is a strong plea for 'correct translations . . . into different languages . . . from the original texts', made if possible in co-operation with the separated brethren. The Dogmatic Constitution on Divine Revelation (par. 12) declares that no interpreter can discover what God wants to say in Scripture without first studying what the human author wanted to say, with due attention to his style and cultural background.

All this, however, is superficial in comparison with the central affirmation of the document on Divine Revelation that 'sacred tradition and sacred Scripture form one sacred deposit of the word of God, which is committed to the church' (par. 10). What this means is that the revelation of God in Jesus Christ is known to us through the apostolic tradition, which was in its entirety committed to writing in the New Testament, but which was also in its entirety entrusted by the apostles to their successors in perpetuity, as a living tradition in the Church, with Pope and bishops, the *magisterium*, as its authoritative guardians.

The apostolic preaching, which is expressed in a special way in the inspired books, was to be preserved by a continuous succession of preachers until the end of time. Therefore the apostles, handing on what they themselves had received, warn the faithful to hold fast to the traditions which they have learned either by word of mouth or by letter, and to fight in defense of the faith handed on once for all. Now what was handed on by the apostles includes everything which contributes to the holiness of life, and the increase in faith of the People of God; and so the Church, in her teaching, life, and worship, perpetuates and hands on to all generations all that she herself is, all that she believes. (Const. on Divine Revelation, par. 8.)

Many critics of the Council have expressed regret that the document did not include an explicit declaration of academic freedom for Roman Catholic scholars, and their fear that the new doctrine might be interpreted in a repressive sense. Roman exegetes, they suppose, are free to find in Scripture only what the cumulative tradition and the present state of episcopal opinion allow them to find. This I consider to be an unwarranted anxiety. There may be no guarantee of academic freedom, but there is an explicit statement that 'the *magisterium* is not above the word of God, but serves it.' It is for the bishops to declare to the Church and to the world what is the Catholic faith, and no scholar or theologian has the right to contradict his bishop on that subject on the grounds that he can justify his opinion out of Scripture. But he has both the right and the duty to pursue his biblical studies with complete integrity and dedication to the cause of truth, so that through his work the bishop may be enabled to discharge his office as servant of the Word; or, to put it in words I have already quoted in my first

lecture, 'so that through preparatory study the judgment of
the Church may mature'. I cannot see that even a Protestant
scholar could ask for a fairer deal than that. I consider myself
free to pursue my studies (in such time as I have left over from
other duties) and to publish them (if I wish to do so and can
find a publisher) as my own personal opinion, for what it is
worth; but I have no right to offer my work to the world as
though it were an agreed statement of the faith of the
Congregational Church.

It is of course easy enough to find examples of Roman
Catholic exegesis in which dogma and not unfettered scholar-
ship appears to be in control. Not long ago the Catholic
hierarchy in Great Britain announced their intention of adopt-
ing the Revised Standard Version of the Bible as their official
English translation, provided they were allowed to make some
slight alterations. The slight alterations have proved to include
one in the story of the Annunciation and one in the story of the
epileptic boy. According to the R.S.V., Gabriel's greeting to
Mary was, 'Hail, O favoured one!'; and the Catholic revision
has restored from the Latin Vulgate the reading, 'full of grace',
which can hardly be regarded as a possible rendering of the
Greek. Where in the R.S.V. Jesus says, 'This kind cannot be
driven out by anything but prayer', the Catholic revision adds,
'and fasting'—a reading widely attested, but not in the earliest
manuscripts, on which all modern critical editions of the Greek
text are based, including that of the Jesuit Merk, who includes
these words only in square brackets. But even if in these and
other instances we may suspect the influence of dogmatic
considerations, this does not necessarily imply that the scholars
concerned have been robbed of academic freedom by ecclesiastical discipline. There is the other possibility that these scholars

sincerely believe the teaching of their Church, so that it acts upon them by inner conviction and not by external constraint.

This is a phenomenon with which we all have personal acquaintance, though some are more ready to admit it than others. We all tend to interpret Scripture in the light of and in the interests of our deepest convictions. The most notorious fact about the history of Protestantism is that all Protestants have appealed to the sole authority of Scripture, but by that sole authority have contrived to justify a variety of contradictory theological positions (e.g. infant baptism and adult baptism), and an even greater variety of mutually incompatible systems of church order. Already in the seventeenth century this drew caustic comment from the Swiss scholar Werenfels.

> Hic liber est in quo quaerit sua dogmata quisque,
> Invenit et pariter dogmata quisque sua.

('This is the book in which every man searches for his own opinions, and every man with equal success finds his own opinions.') The chief reason why the Church of Rome still thinks fit to retain some ecclesiastical control over the interpretation of Scripture is that this has seemed the only alternative to total chaos. There was a time when many Protestants felt it necessary to exercise just as tight a control over both ministers and laity, and to exact from them submission to a rigid confessionalism; and there are some denominations where this practice still survives, whether openly or through the control of key appointments. Most of us, however, have come round to the belief that the only proper safeguards against a rampant subjectivism are free academic debate, ruthless self-discipline in the examination of our own presuppositions, and, not least, a renewed confidence in the ability of God to watch over his

Word. What I have been trying to suggest is that Rome has now taken some decisive steps in the same direction.

In this persuasion I propose to spend the rest of this lecture discussing five questions about the use of Scripture which occurred to me as I read through the documents of Vatican II, not because I think we are in a position to dictate the answers, but because dialogue with Rome gives us an opportunity to take a fresh look at matters essential to our own faith and order.

1. *Proof Text and Context*

A visitor to the Zoo met a man who was running towards him in great agitation and shouting, 'There's a moose loose!' With some presence of mind the visitor asked, 'Are you English or Scottish?' It is hardly possible to frame a sentence which could not be given more than one meaning if it appeared in different contexts. If we want to know the meaning of any statement, we must know who said it and in what circumstances. Words, as Humpty Dumpty pointed out, mean exactly what the speaker or writer intends them to mean, neither more nor less. Now a proof text is a verse of Scripture cited as an authority in support of an argument, but without reference to its context. When all Christians, Catholic or Protestant, assumed that every word of the Bible was inspired by God and dictated by the Holy Spirit, I suppose there was some propriety in the use of proof texts, since each separate utterance could be regarded as an oracle from heaven. But undoubtedly this practice was the primary cause of that chaos to which I was alluding just now, in which advocates of warring systems justified their opposite claims from the one Bible. Now that we have come to treat the Bible as a collection of historical documents, to be interpreted in the light of their historical setting and the intention of their authors, we can see that the New Testament does not give unequivocal support to any one of the forms of church order that have been discovered in it, for the simple reason that its writers did not share the passionate interest in this subject evinced by leaders of the Ecumenical Movement. But you can prove almost any case by a judicious selection of evidence.

The Vatican Council has now firmly discarded the proof-text method as a misuse of Scripture. 'Since God speaks in sacred Scripture through men in human fashion, the interpreter of sacred Scripture, in order to see clearly what God wanted to communicate to us, should carefully investigate what meaning the sacred writers intended.' (Const. on Divine Revelation, par. 12.) If God speaks through the writers of Scripture, he speaks not only through their lips but through their minds. He does not indulge in double-talk, allowing Isaiah or Paul to mean one thing by what they say, while he himself means another.

If this admirable principle were consistently carried through, we should soon find that differences of opinion about the meaning of Scripture, though they would undoubtedly occur, would no longer be drawn along party lines. But our own experience ought to warn us that there is always a time-lag between the recognition of a new principle and its consistent application in practice. There is an inevitable tension between newly accepted truth and long treasured assumptions. We must not then be either irritated or unduly dismayed to find that the Vatican documents all too frequently lapse into the proof-text technique. Many of these documents are essentially pastoral in their scope and intention, and their use of Scripture is illustrative rather than doctrinally binding. I therefore limit myself to three examples from the Dogmatic Constitution on the Church, which is one of the two documents carrying real doctrinal authority.

(a) The third chapter first asserts that bishops are successors to the apostles, and then adds that 'for the discharging of such great duties, the apostles were enriched by Christ with a special outpouring of the Holy Spirit.' If this statement had been supported by a reference to 1 Corinthians 12.28, where Paul lists apostleship as the first of the charismatic gifts of the Spirit, I should have no quarrel with it. But in fact the theological commission has chosen to cite Acts 1.8 and 2.4. These texts are obviously being taken to mean that the outpouring of the Spirit on the apostles at Pentecost and the status which they were therefore able to transmit to their successors was in some way different in kind from the outpouring of the Spirit on ordinary Christians at baptism. Now it is true that Acts 1.8 records a promise of Jesus to the eleven surviving apostles that they are to receive the Spirit and be his witnesses to the ends of the earth. But in the rest of the book only Peter, James, and John are mentioned by name, and the task of world-wide witness is in fact carried out by others, with no suggestion that they were authorized to do so by anyone except the Holy Spirit himself. Luke clearly regarded the Twelve not as the prototype of an ordained ministry, but as the symbolic nucleus of the whole people of God. When the promised Spirit descends at Pentecost, Peter makes it clear that he regards this as a fulfilment of God's promise, given through the prophet Joel, to pour out his Spirit on all mankind, and that precisely the same gift of the Spirit is available for all who will call upon the name of the Lord and be baptized. We are debarred from saying that, in the mind of Luke, the apostles had a special grace, in that only they could communicate the gift of the Spirit to others through the laying on of hands, because later in the story Paul is said to receive the Spirit through the laying on of hands by Ananias. To cite these texts, then, as evidence for 'a special outpouring' is to ignore the intentions of the human author.

(b) The next section of the same chapter expounds the new doctrine of collegiality. Plenary authority resides not simply in the Pope, but in the college of bishops with the Pope at their head. The chief scriptural argument for this is that 'the power of binding and loosing, which was given to Peter (Matt. 16.19), was granted also to the college of apostles, joined with their head (Matt. 18.18).' Now it is beyond question that the words of Jesus about binding and loosing occur twice in Matthew's Gospel, though few commentators are prepared to give a decisive opinion about their meaning, and it is not even certain whether it is preferable to be bound or loosed. But let us grant that some sort of authority is here being conferred. The question is, On whom? At the beginning of Matthew 18 we are told that Jesus was talking to his disciples. This is not in itself an answer to our question, since Matthew does not as clearly as Mark distinguish between the Twelve on the one hand and the larger group of disciples on the other; so that when he says 'disciples', he might mean the one or the other. But there is a simple test for determining which he meant here. He has collected in this chapter a large number of sayings of Jesus, and presumably means us to understand that they were all addressed to the same audience. Now the saying immediately preceding the one at issue runs like this. 'If your brother sins against you, go and tell him his fault, between you and him alone. If he listens to you, you have gained your brother. But if he does not listen, take one or two others along with you, that every word may be confirmed by the evidence of two or three witnesses. If he refuses to listen to them, tell it to the church.' Was Jesus here prescribing for the settlement of quarrels on the episcopal bench? If so, he was putting quarrelsome bishops very firmly under the authority of the church meeting. Surely it is obvious that Matthew meant this teaching to apply to the whole Christian community. But then it follows inescapably that he understood the authority to bind and loose to be vested in the whole Christian community. However admirable may be the principle of episcopal collegiality, it gains no support from this particular text, which demonstrably has nothing whatever to do with either apostles or bishops.

(c) The seventh chapter of the same document deals with 'the eschatological nature of the pilgrim church and her union with the heavenly church'; and in this connexion it commends the practice of offering prayers for the dead. There was a time when 'prayers for the dead' would have been fighting words in any Protestant gathering. The brevity and restraint with which this subject is touched upon are eloquent testimony to the desire of the Council Fathers not to reopen old wounds. They commend the practice of praying for the dead on the ground that it forms a bond of union between the church below and the church above. I am bound to say that, put in this light, the practice seems to me both natural and unobjectionable, little removed from the ethos of that portion of our hymnbooks which is concerned with the communion of saints; and I wonder whether we ought not to admit that our fathers, in reacting against the mediaeval doctrine of merit and indulgences, may at this point have reacted too far. But such meditations are harshly interrupted by a quotation from 2 Maccabees, which is supposed to supply the practice of praying for the dead with its sole scriptural authority. Judas Maccabaeus considered it a holy and pious thing to pray for the dead. Even if I were prepared to adopt these very words of Judas, it is plain that I should not be meaning by them what he meant, or what the author of 2 Maccabees meant. For this is not all that Judas is said to have done for that group of Jewish renegades for whom he was praying. He also collected a large sum of money to provide a sin offering, in the persuasion that the offering and the prayers together would atone for the idolatry which he believed had brought them to their untimely death. His reliance on the merits and atoning efficacy of human acts of piety was precisely that form of Judaism which Paul was later to repudiate as incompatible with the gospel of God's all-sufficient grace. It seems therefore a pity to appeal to the example of Judas at a time when merit and the book-keeping type of religion associated with it are rapidly dropping out of the religious vocabulary and practice of Rome.

2. *The Unity of Scripture*

A second principle of biblical interpretation enunciated at Vatican II has to do with the unity of the Bible. 'Since holy Scripture must be read and interpreted according to the same Spirit by whom it was written, no less serious attention must be given to the content and unity of the whole of Scripture.' (Const. on Divine Revelation. par. 12). This is a statement which would have warmed the hearts of the Reformers, for it was one of their cardinal tenets that Scripture must be interpreted in the light of Scripture. *Scriptura scripturae interpres.* This principle would seem to be exactly the corrective needed to the proof-text mentality about which I have just been speaking. The difficulty is that, as soon as you attempt to apply the principle, it proves to be ambiguous. There is one way of taking it which I should consider admirable and another which I should consider disastrous. It all depends on the kind of unity you attribute to the Bible.

If we say that a biblical text must be interpreted in the light of the whole teaching of the Bible, this could mean that we were putting the writers of Scripture on a bed of Procrustes and reducing them to a dull uniformity. Anyone who reads at all widely in the works of Martin Luther cannot but be astonished at the skill with which he discovered the doctrine of justification by faith in the most unlikely parts of the Old Testament; and it is well known that in his earlier writings he summarily dismissed both the Epistle of James and the Revelation of John on the grounds that they did not preach the gospel which he found supremely exemplified in the Epistles to the Romans and the Galatians. More recently there have been scholars so determined to baptize the Old Testament into the Christian faith that by allegory and typology they have reduced it to a vast cryptogram, which conveyed obscurely only what could be plainly read in the Gospel of Mark; and one is left wondering why it ever had to be written at all. The Old Testament authors have important things to say to us in their own right, and they must be allowed to speak for themselves, not turned into pale echoes of the evangelists. Again, if the four Gospels spoke with a single voice, what need would we have of four? In the second century a Syrian called Tatian produced a conflation of the four Gospels into a single continuous narrative, his Diatessaron or Four-in-one, which for a time enjoyed immense popularity; but the Church in the end returned to the four separate Gospels. The real unity of the New Testament is not that all its writers thought alike, but that all their voices are needed in the choir that is to do justice to the central figure of Christ. The proper question to ask about the Book of Revelation is not whether it teaches justification by faith, nor even whether its doctrine is identical with that of Paul or the Fourth Evangelist, but whether the heavenly Lamb and the victorious horseman can be identified with the Jesus of Nazareth known to us in the Gospels. We may well believe that the Holy Spirit does not contradict himself, but we must also allow him the freedom to give us, through many different spokesmen, a great variety of facets of that many-splendoured truth which is bigger than the minds of us all.

3. The Language of Scripture

My third point concerns the language of the Bible. To take the Bible seriously is not the same thing as taking it literally, for much of its teaching is conveyed in picture language, imagery, and figures of speech. Pius XII had already written at length on this subject in his encyclical *Divino Afflante Spiritu*, so that it is no surprise to find the Council Fathers following his lead and affirming that an accurate interpretation of the Bible depends on a full understanding of its linguistic conventions and literary forms. The Dogmatic Constitution on the Church, as well as that on Divine Revelation, draws attention to the figurative nature of biblical language. 'In the Old Testament the revelation of the kingdom had often been conveyed by figures of speech. In the same way the inner nature of the Church was now to be made known to us through various images' (par. 6). There follows a detailed treatment of four metaphors: the Church as the flock of Christ, as the vineyard of God, as the temple of the Holy Spirit, and as the Spouse of the Immaculate Lamb. You will notice that from this list there is one conspicuous omission. The Church as the body of Christ is dealt with at length elsewhere in the Constitution, but it is not here included among the list of metaphors. I can only deduce from this that the authors of this document did not think of this description of the Church as a metaphor, and in this view they would find some small body of support outside their own communion. For my part I have always looked upon this attitude with astonishment and regret: astonishment, because when Paul uses this expression it is often not even a metaphor but a simile; and regret, because I detect here a reluctance to admit the figurative nature of all religious language. This reluctance is not, of course, confined to Roman Catholics. When Rudolf Bultmann invited us to demythologize the New Testament, he was really asking us to dispense with picture language and to express ourselves wholly in the language of philosophical abstraction, which he fancied would be more acceptable to the modern man-in-the-street; not recognizing that even philosophical abstractions are abstracted from the concreteness of pictures, without which it is not possible for us to talk about God at all. The second commandment forbad the Jews to make a graven image, but they amply compensated for this prohibition with the wealth of their verbal imagery.

One of the most interesting examples of the complications we can get into through failing to distinguish the different levels of language we are using is provided by Chapter VIII of the Dogmatic Constitution on the Church, which is devoted to the Virgin Mary. This chapter traces Catholic veneration of Mary back to biblical foundations in the Old Testament as well as in the New. We are reminded that in the Old Testament we frequently read of an ideal figure called the Daughter of Sion, sometimes the virgin Daughter of Sion. This ideal woman is clearly a symbol for the city of Jerusalem or for the people of God, and it is no surprise that this virgin turns out also to be the mother of a large family of children. (No mention is made of the many other passages in the Old Testament where the same figure of speech is used to refer to other cities, such as 'the virgin daughter of Babylon'.) This Daughter of Sion, we are told, is to be identified with the virgin mother of Immanuel in the prophecy of Isaiah, and reappears in the New Testament in Paul's reference to the Jerusalem that is above, who is mother of us all, and in the vision which John of Patmos saw of a woman clothed with the sun and crowned with the stars, who gave birth to a male child. This mother figure of the Old Testament 'prophetically foreshadowed' the motherhood of Mary.

At this point it is proper for the Protestant to pause and ask himself whether, in his revulsion against what he took to be the idolatrous practices of Rome, he has not turned his back on a wealth of biblical imagery that might have been used to stimulate the imagination and feed the soul. For here we are dealing not merely with imagery, but with archetypal imagery, imagery that belongs to the permanent and universal furniture of the human mind. In an age in which imagination is dying of famine, we do well to make a long-range survey of available food supplies.

What is happening in the Roman account of their devotion to Mary, however, is not just the adornment of the Mother of Jesus with some splendid metaphors. It is something more complex than that. Jesus has two mothers, one literal, the other metaphorical: literally he is son of Mary, metaphorically son of the Daughter of Sion. What Rome has done is to identify these two figures in such a way that the attributes of the one are wholly transferable to the other. In so doing they claim to have early and authoritative precedent. Luke in his nativity story has treated Mary as a representative person, who in the Magnificat speaks not for herself alone but for the whole expectant people of God; and Irenaeus in the second century was already speaking of Mary as the second Eve, whose obedience had undone the disobedience of her first mother.

On this I have three comments to make. The first is that Luke portrays Mary as representative of a real, earthly, historical, and very human community of which she herself was a member; but Catholic devotion has tended to identify Mary with the idealized Daughter of Sion, the heavenly rather than the earthly Jerusalem. My second comment is that much can properly be expressed in the poetry of worship and devotion which will not bear logical analysis or reduction to the cold prose of dogma. You will understand that I have not been attempting to examine the case for or against the three Marian dogmas propounded by the Church of Rome. What I am saying is that, before ever we approach that thorny tangle, there are questions about biblical imagery and the language of religion to which we must give a great deal of thought. Is it ever legitimate to argue from the metaphorical to the literal or vice versa? That the poet's mind freely ranges by precisely this type of associative thinking cannot for a moment be disputed.

My third comment is of a different kind. We Protestants cannot be too grateful for the courage and generosity with which the Council Fathers have grasped this particular nettle. They have recognized what a serious obstacle their Mariology has been to Protestants, and they could hardly have done more to allay our suspicions without seriously imperilling the simple faith of millions of loyal Catholics. Whatever residual doubts we may have, we can have a real sympathy with a portrayal of Mary which puts all the emphasis on her role as a member of the Church who shares with other members the need of redemption, and as a symbol of the Church's present faith and future glory. But anyone who has lived in a Catholic country and seen the cult of Mary at first hand as it is conducted among unsophisticated folk cannot help but wonder what all this has to do with the day-to-day piety of the parish churches of Sicily and Quebec, of Lima, Bangalore, Jakarta, and Manila. Does it not look a little bit like rationalization, the attempt to give respectable reasons for practices that originated from less exalted sources? The answer is that such transvaluation is to be observed in the history of almost all religious symbols and ceremonies. Symbols and ceremonies long outlive the impulse that brought them into being. As Dr. Austin Farrer has so forcefully explained to us, there can be a 'rebirth of images'; old symbols and images can be reborn, reminted to a new currency as vehicles of new sentiments and meanings. The best possible illustration is provided by the history of the central rite in the Christian religion. It began its existence as the spring festival in the lunar cult of a group of pastoral nomads; it was transformed by Moses into an annual commemoration of God's redemptive act in bringing Israel out of slavery in Egypt, and so became the Jewish Passover; and centuries later in an upper room it underwent a further rebirth of images to become the Christian Eucharist. If, as I suspect, we have witnessed the beginnings of a rebirth in the Roman cult of Mary, perhaps it is the counsel of prudence that we outsiders should not cause it to miscarry by asking too many awkward questions.

Before I leave this question of language and imagery, I should like to recall to you a passage from last year's lectures, in which John Huxtable added new lustre to this series. Those who heard or have read the lectures (*Christian Unity: Some of the Issues*, Independent Press, London) will recall that he raised important questions about the use of the word 'priest'. The English word is etymologically derived from the Latin *presbyter*, but it is also the standard translation of the Latin *sacerdos*. In the documents of Vatican II both words are freely used in the Latin text, and they are both represented in the English translation by the only available equivalent. The Dogmatic Constitution on the Church, for example, cites the biblical evidence for the existence of priests (*presbyteri*) in the New Testament period, and then continues: 'let the bishop regard his priests (*sacerdotes*) . . . as sons and friends' (par. 28). Now it is incontrovertible that in later times these two Latin words came to be exact synonyms. But in New Testament times the Greek word *presbyteros* denoted an office which had no priestly functions. The language of priesthood, apart from one or two obviously figurative uses, was employed only of the unique and unrepeatable priesthood of Christ and of the priestly calling of the whole community. In the first two centuries the presbyter had no special connexion even with the liturgy, let alone with a sacerdotal interpretation of it. My point again is that, before we can profitably come to the discussion of deep doctrinal differences, we need to do a great deal of hard thinking together about the semantics of biblical language.

4. *Scripture and Tradition*

When the *schema* on the two sources of revelation was withdrawn and a new draft document introduced, which declared that Scripture and tradition are not separate sources of revelation, but different forms in which the one deposit of faith has been transmitted, the immediate reaction of all Protestants was to rejoice that one of the major barriers between us had been thrown down. That, I believe, is still the proper response; but there is another side to the matter. In the debate on this document the conservatives asked a question which we observers also wanted to ask, though perhaps for different reasons. 'Does this mean that there are now no dogmas of the church which are based on tradition alone?' Amongst others was Archbishop Attipetty of Verapoly in India. 'If it is not clearly reaffirmed', he said, 'that tradition alone, without relationship to Scripture, is also a source of revelation, it would mean that everything that has until now been proclaimed as dogma will now officially be declared false. If no stand is taken on this point, the Church will bring ridicule upon herself, as though she had hitherto taught a false doctrine. There would also be ridicule for those dogmas, such as the bodily Assumption of Mary into heaven, which are based solely upon tradition.' In spite of such eloquent appeals, no answer to the question was given. But obviously the matter cannot be for long left where it is. The Church of Rome has abandoned the solid ground of her logical, mediaeval system, and is now standing on one leg on a stepping-stone; she must either go back or go on. If she goes on, there would seem to be only two possible courses. Either she must say, 'The development of tradition *can* add nothing to the one deposit of faith; therefore we must abjure, or at least consign to oblivion, any teaching which is clearly unscriptural'; or she must say, 'The development of tradition *has* added nothing to the deposit of faith; and we must prove this by methods of exegesis which will discover biblical justification for those teachings which hitherto we had been content to base on tradition alone.'

I make no attempt to disguise my strong conviction that, if the Church of Rome were to adopt the second course, this would be unmitigated tragedy. What is at stake here is very close to the heart of our Christian religion. The one thing that distinguishes Christianity from all other religions and philosophies is that it is in the first instance neither a set of doctrines nor a way of life, but a gospel; and a gospel means news about historical events, attested by reliable witnesses, and having at their centre an historical person. The first two heresies the church had to face in the second century were Docetism, which denied the real, historical existence of Christ, and Gnosticism, which undermined even more comprehensively the distinction between history and speculation. Whenever Christians have attempted to give to the Scriptures a sense other than the plain sense intended by the men who wrote them, Christianity has been in danger of running out into the sands of Gnosticism. And the danger is at its greatest when dogma or philosophical presuppositions are allowed to take control of exegesis.

This danger is not confined to Roman Catholics. We Protestants and our fathers before us have been living through a long period of scepticism about the historicity of our biblical records. My own belief is that this scepticism is not the inevitable product of objective historic research; for, whenever secular historians have set their minds to the biblical evidence, they have commonly come to far more conservative conclusions than the theologians. Sceptical results have been accepted in what seems to me a naïvely uncritical fashion, because they were congenial to the dogmatic presuppositions of the researcher. If, for example, you believe that faith is not faith which can find support in anything other than the unconditioned grace of God, you will be predisposed to welcome the discovery that historic research cannot intrude upon that utter faith by proving beyond reasonable doubt any single fact about the person of Jesus.

Anyone who believes in the Incarnation, whether he be Catholic or Protestant, and whether he likes it or not, is committed to the quest of the historical Jesus; and any method of handling Scripture which blunts the tools of that quest must be regarded as a disservice to the gospel.

Nothing I have said should be taken as a criticism of the principles of scriptural interpretation laid down in the Dogmatic Constitution on Divine Revelation. They are admirable, and, if they are taken seriously, we have nothing to fear. The question is whether they will be strong enough to bear the strain that will be put upon them when Catholic theologians attempt an answer to that very awkward conundrum about the relation of dogma to the one deposit of faith, which is now said to be the content alike of Scripture and tradition.

5. The Authors of Scripture

My final question, which I shall pose without stopping to develop it, concerns the authors of Scripture, human and divine. Besides drawing attention to the importance of the human author, his style, conventions, and presuppositions, the documents of Vatican II frequently refer to God or to the Holy

Spirit as the author of the Bible. This form of speech, though found in the records of sixteenth and seventeenth century Protestantism, is no longer current among us; but we do still regularly speak of the Bible as the Word of God, which I take to be much the same thing. I wonder, however, whether the Council Fathers were any clearer in their minds about this dual authorship than we are. At one point they draw an analogy between it and the existence of two natures in the one person of Christ. 'The words of God, expressed in human language, have been made like human discourse, just as of old the Word of the eternal Father, when he took to Himself the weak flesh of humanity, became like other men.' (Const. on Divine Revelation, par. 13.) I find this impressive but unilluminating; and I cannot help recalling that it took the Church over four centuries to settle its ideas about the two natures of Christ. The advent of biblical criticism has relieved us of many naïve ideas and misapprehensions about the Bible, and has supplied us with a vast amount of knowledge about its compilation and background. All this has beyond question made us more accurate interpreters of Scripture, but it has apparently not made it easier for ordinary Christians to read it, let alone to read it as the Word of God. The vision of Erasmus has not yet come true in this twentieth century of ours. No item on the agenda of our dialogue with Rome seems to me more urgent than this, that we should together think through the way in which human authorship and divine word are related to one another, so that we may put the Bible back into the hand of the wayfaring pilgrim to use as the chief of his means of grace.

3. *The Nature of Authority*

THERE was once a village which voted that the earth was flat. It would have made no difference if the vote had been taken in a more authoritative legislature—the Assembly of the Congregational Church, the Vatican Council, or the United Nations. There is an authority inherent in the truth which is neither increased by man's assent nor diminished by his contradiction. Like the lady who irritated Thomas Carlyle, we had better accept the universe.

'The report was true,' said the Queen of Sheba, 'which I heard of your affairs and of your wisdom, but I did not believe the reports until I came and my own eyes had seen it; and, behold, the half was not told me.' There is an authority in personal experience for which second-hand information, however well attested, is a poor substitute; and though in daily life we often have to take things on trust, because life is too short and our talents too limited for us to be experts in everything, there is no room for second-hand religion. 'I know him whom I have believed.'

A young schoolmaster, watching a senior colleague wade into a riot of small boys and quell it with a few well-chosen words, exclaimed, 'I wish I could do that!' There is an authority a man brings to his office, as well as an authority he derives from his office. 'I may' does not guarantee 'I can.'

'The Pope's little finger is stronger than all Germany,' said the Cardinal Legate to Martin Luther. 'Do you expect your princes to take up arms to defend *you*—you, a wretched worm like you? I tell you, No! and where will you be then, where will you be then?' 'Then as now,' said Luther, 'in the hands of Almighty God.'

These four illustrations may not cover all the possible meanings of authority, but they should serve to remind us that the concept of authority is as complex as any with which the human mind has to grapple. It is important to recognize this at the outset, because the past failure of communication between Catholic and Protestant has been due in no small measure to oversimplification of the problems of authority on both sides of the debate. The dogma of Papal infallibility brought to a head a long-standing tendency in the Church of Rome to locate all authority in a hierarchical structure, and to dismiss any departure from the ecclesiastical norm with the dictum that error has no rights. Protestants, on the other hand, tended to find the last court of appeal in the individual judgement or conscience. 'It belongs to each and every Christian,' said Luther, 'to judge of doctrine, and belongs in such wise that he is anathema who shall have diminished this right by a single hair.' With slightly more theological depth and less picturesque language Calvin ascribed this right of the individual Christian to the inner witness of the Holy Spirit. Neither of them would have wanted to quarrel with Coleridge's epigrammatic summary: 'Whatever finds me is the Word of God.' No doubt these descriptions of Catholic and Protestant are caricatures, but they certainly represent the view that each had of the other. I do not propose to make them more accurate, for we are concerned not with the past but with the present. Whatever difficulties we Protestants may have had in the past with what we were pleased to think of as the authoritarian regime of Rome, we now have to come to terms with the fact that in at least three distinct ways Vatican II has modified not only the image that Rome presents to the world, but her own understanding of the nature of religious authority.

(a) *Religious Liberty*. The Declaration of Religious Liberty is a proclamation to the world of the belief of the Catholic Church that a man has an inalienable right 'to be immune from coercion on the part of individuals or of social groups and of any human power,' which might either force him 'to act in a manner contrary to his own beliefs,' or might restrain him 'from acting in accordance with his own beliefs, whether privately or publicly, whether alone or in association with others, within due limits' (par. 2). Fears were expressed in the Council that any limitation of this right might give a loophole to repressive governments, and so the limits had to be carefully defined. Only when there is a breach of public order, or when liberty is so abused as to infringe the liberty of others, is the civil power entitled to intervene. Our interest, however, lies in the two reasons given for this declaration of rights. The first is said to be inherent in the nature of man. All men have the duty to seek the truth and to submit to its obligations once they have found it. But 'the truth cannot impose itself except by virtue of its own truth, as it makes its entrance into the mind at once quietly and with power' (par. 1). 'As truth is discovered, it is by a personal assent that men are to adhere to it' (par. 3). In particular, 'the exercise of religion consists before all else in those internal, voluntary, and free acts whereby man sets the course of his life directly toward God' (ibid.). During the debate on this document a number of speakers demanded that the Church should reiterate her old war-cry that 'error has no rights', since truth exercises a binding obligation on all. The answer came back: 'Certainly error has no rights, but neither does truth, or any other abstraction; only persons have rights, and they have the same rights whether they are in truth or in error.' The right to freedom is inherent in man's nature and is therefore never forfeited, even if a man should refuse to use his freedom in the search for and the service of truth. The second reason is theological. 'It is one of the major tenets of Catholic doctrine that man's response to God in faith must be free.' Where there is coercion, there may be obedience, but there cannot be faith. 'The act of faith is of its very nature a free act. Man, redeemed by Christ the Saviour and through Christ Jesus called to be God's adopted son, cannot give his adherence to God revealing himself unless the Father draw him to offer to God the reasonable and free submission of faith' (par. 10).

The terms in which man's right to civil liberty is affirmed can hardly fail to have repercussions on life within the Church itself. You might well be pardoned for wondering whether the quotations I have given you come from a Catholic document or from some modern version of Luther's *Treatise on Christian Liberty*. In the past the Church of Rome has given the impression that by faith she meant unquestioning acceptance of her own authoritative teaching, that she was treating her adherents as children, and if they were to have the temerity to ask, 'Why?', the answer would be, 'Because Mother says so.' Whether that was a correct impression or not, there can be no doubt now that Mother Church is demanding from her children an adult faith, a direct response to God for which they must accept full personal responsibility. They are to be 'lovers of true freedom —men, in other words, who will come to decisions on their own judgment and in the light of truth, govern their activities with a sense of responsibility, and strive after what is true and right, willing always to join with others in co-operative effort' (par. 8).

This is not what is commonly thought of as Protestant individualism, but it comes very near to what P. T. Forsyth taught us nearly fifty years ago. It was he who reminded us that, though conscience may be the seat of authority, it is not its source: conscience is the subjective faculty by which we recognize and submit to an authority which is in itself objective. He also warned us that we could have no answer to Papal infallibility unless Protestant freedom could prove itself capable of more radical obedience to the claims of the gospel than was possible under an authoritarian discipline. But there is a third point which I think even Forsyth overlooked. The Vatican declaration makes much of the fact than a man cannot be religious except in community, and that therefore he must have freedom of corporate action and expression. But this means that a man's individual response to God, however important that may be, cannot even be the only *seat* of authority in the church.

This could be so only if we were prepared to commit ourselves to a 'social contract' view of the church. Congregationalists are accustomed to speak of covenanting. Christians in any given locality covenant together to form a church. Their local churches have just covenanted together to form a single Congregational Church in England and Wales. They are, I trust, on the point of covenanting with the Presbyterians to unite the Congregational and Presbyterian Churches. It may be that this notion of covenanting will provide the formula for further union. But those who speak of covenanting have never supposed that they were the originators of the covenant. The covenant has its source in the elective love and mercy of God, who first called the nation of Israel into being, then, in a new covenant, sealed in the lifeblood of Christ, created a new people of God transcending national and all other human barriers. Our covenanting, then, is no social contract between hitherto isolated individuals, each the captain of his fate and master of his soul, but rather our acknowledgement that we are already by God's call and grace the local manifestation of the universal church which he has brought into being in Christ.

(b) *Institutional and Spiritual Authority.* If two men or two teams wish to play a game, it is well that they should first agree on the rules. The M.C.C. may alter the rules of cricket, but not during a Test Match. A golfer may come to a gentlemen's agreement with his opponent about what to do if a ball is caught in a gorse bush, but, if he wishes to keep his friends, he will not take unilateral action. Rules are rules until they are changed. On the other hand, when William Webb Ellis picked up the ball and ran with it on the playing field of Rugby, he introduced a change in the rules of football so radical that he actually invented a new, and greatly superior, game. What is true of games holds also for all human societies and institutions. All require rules of procedure if they are not to grind to a halt; but some of the rules are integral to their nature and purpose, others are matters of mutual convenience and agreement. A Dramatic Society may have many peculiar rules about membership, officers, subscriptions, and meetings; but, if it decides never to perform or even read a play, it has clearly changed its essential character. Similarly a church has some characteristics, such as worship, without which it would cease to be a church, and others which are only rules of procedure. But where are we to draw the line? Some Protestants believe that church order as a whole exists solely for the sake of orderly procedure, and that the church could order itself otherwise without changing its essential character. At the other extreme there are churches in which the spiritual authority inherent in the church's nature and function and the institutional authority involved in the administration of rules of procedure have been so long vested in the same persons that the distinction I have been making has been blurred.

It is therefore a matter of some importance that Vatican II has clearly and explicitly accepted the distinction. The Decree on the Ministry and Life of Priests, for example, states that celibacy is not 'demanded by the very nature of the priesthood, as is evident from the practice of the primitive church and from the tradition of the Eastern Churches' (par. 16). It is a long-standing law of the Latin Church, and is to be retained because of its usefulness and propriety in the churches which stand in the Latin tradition.

Discussions about where you are to draw the line between rules demanded by the nature of the church and rules of procedure have bulked large in ecumenical debate. Without denying that this is a proper and important question, I should say that the Council Fathers were right to devote a very considerable part of their time and energies to an allied and more urgent question, which in some degree presses upon us all. How can you prevent institutional authority and the bureaucracy that wields it from so magnifying themselves that they eclipse the spiritual authority which is integral to the Church's nature, and so become determinative for the life and character of the Church? To put it bluntly, how can you stop the referee blowing the whistle so often that nobody on the field has a chance to play the game?

This was the real point at issue behind the lengthy discussion on the collegial authority of bishops. The conservatives tried to make out that this was a straight fight between Pope and bishops, between a traditional monarchy and a new-fangled aristocracy—a sort of Roman Runnymede in which the ecclesiastical barons were attempting to extort from the sovereign a Magna Carta Catholica. Since the Pope was clearly on the side of the bishops, this was a superficial and unrealistic estimate of the situation. The real question before the Church was whether the Pope's authority was to be interpreted as a governmental and legalistic authority exercised through the Curia or as a spiritual and pastoral authority exercised in conjunction with his brother bishops. Nobody questions that an institution as large as the Catholic Church— larger than most of the sovereign states which comprise the United Nations—needs a civil service. The question is how far the Church as an institution can afford to conform to the institutional patterns of the world. Even in civil governments, a new cabinet minister must often have the frustrating experience of being told by the Permanent Head of his Ministry that the policies he proposes are administratively unsound, and that he must bow to expert knowledge.

We do not need a Parkinson to enunciate for us a law of ecclesiastical authority. Jesus repeatedly warned the Pharisees that anyone engrossed in formulating and enforcing ecclesiastical rules was likely to lose sight of the weightier matters of religious observance. Spiritual life requires a spontaneity which is not amenable to regimentation. That the modern Roman Catholic is aware of this danger is apparent from the frequency with which, in conversation, the word 'sinister' occurs in reference to the activities of the Holy See. In the Council debate on collegiality one speaker argued that the time had come to do away with such officials as Apostolic Nuncios and Delegates, whom he described as 'shadows hiding the genuine face of the Church'. Their presence in a country suggested that the Church was aping secular powers and meddling in international politics; and the representation of the Church in any country would be better left to the bishops, who were in a position to know their people more intimately than an outsider. This proposal subsequently found an echo in the Decree on the Pastoral Office of Bishops:

In exercising supreme, full, and immediate power over the universal church, the Roman Pontiff makes use of the departments of the Roman Curia. These, therefore, perform their duties in his name and with his authority for the good of the churches and for the service of the sacred pastors. The Fathers of this most sacred Council, however, strongly desire that these departments—which have rendered exceptional assistance to the Roman Pontiff and to the pastors of the Church—be reorganized and better adapted to the needs of the times, and of various regions and rites. This task should give special thought to their number, name, competence, and particular method of procedure, as well as to the coordination of their activities. The Fathers also eagerly desire that, in view of the pastoral role proper to bishops, the office of legates of the Roman Pontiff be more precisely determined (par. 9).

A Papal Commission, under the chairmanship of Cardinal Roberti, has been charged with the duty of making recommendations about the reform of the Roman Curia. The Pope has announced the formation of a new Synod of Bishops, which is an attempt to give structural expression to the conviction that the policies of the Church must be controlled by its spiritual and pastoral nature and not by its administrative machine. Equally important is the newly defined sacramental nature of episcopal consecration. Bishops are appointed by the Pope and may not exercise their authority without his consent, but they do not derive their authority from him. They are in no sense his delegates. Their authority comes to them directly from Christ's appointment of apostles, and is communicated to them through their consecration. Hitherto the Roman Church had believed in a sacrament of ordination, and had held that bishops differed from priests only in possessing superior jurisdiction. Now it is clearly stated that their authority is essentially sacramental, and that the jurisdictional element is secondary.

To Protestants with no experience of or interest in the workings of hierarchy this may seem alien and remote, but to those who take the trouble to learn the language it is a significant and promising change. In the terminology of Vatican II 'sacramental' was the antithesis of 'legalistic'. In the first chapter of the Dogmatic Constitution on the Church the Church itself is described both as a mystery and as a sacrament, and the two terms may be regarded as roughly synonymous. What they mean is that the Church and its ministry exist by God's will as a visible token of his grace and activity and a means by which his presence becomes real to the believer. If we wanted to be awkward, we could ask whether this is in fact the function discharged by bishops in the day-to-day life of the Church of Rome. If you put sacramental and administrative authority into the same hands, then the sheer pressure of practical decisions will always ensure that the administrative squeezes out the sacramental. But at least there is no denying that this new teaching represents a considerable shift of emphasis in Roman thinking about authority.

(c) *Ministerial Authority*. It has been a catchword of Congregationalism that we believe in ministerial authority, not magisterial. In this, I believe, we have made two mistakes. We have construed ministerial authority in such a way that it has frequently ceased to be authority in any sense of the word; and we have overlooked the ambiguity of the Latin word *magister*, which can mean anything from a dictator to a schoolmaster. We have taken magisterial authority to be the right to dominate, and have knocked that Aunt Sally down with well-chosen words from the Gospels about not being like those who lord it over the Gentiles. But when the Roman Catholic Church speaks of Pope and bishops as a *magisterium*, they mean those charged with the responsibility of teaching; and there is no obvious antithesis between that and a ministry properly so-called. We rightly speak of the ministry of Jesus, of whom it was said that he taught with authority.

However this may be, the present position is that the documents of Vatican II constantly revert to the theme of service. 'Those ministers who are endowed with sacred power are servants of their brethren.' (Const. on the Church, par. 18). 'Bishops govern the particular churches entrusted to them as the vicars and ambassadors of Christ. This they do by their counsel, exhortations, and example, as well, indeed, as by their authority and sacred power. This power they use only for the edification of their flock in truth and holiness, remembering that he who is greater should become as the lesser and he who is the more distinguished as the servant (cf. Luke 22.26–27)' (ibid, par. 27). 'Since he is sent by the Father to govern His family, a bishop must keep before his eyes the example of the Good Shepherd, who came not to be ministered unto but to minister (cf. Mark 10.45), and to lay down His life for His sheep (cf. John 10.11)' (ibid.). 'Priests, prudent cooperators with the episcopal order as well as its aids and instruments, are called to serve the People of God. . . . And let the bishop regard his priests, who are his co-workers, as sons and friends, just as Christ called His disciples no longer servants but friends (cf. John 15.15)' (ibid., par. 28). One bishop after another spoke of the need to strip off the mediaeval trappings of worldly pomp and power, and to return to the primitive simplicity of the apostolic church. The *schema* on the Apostolate of the Laity was described by one speaker as 'begotten in sin, the sin of clericalism', because it assumed that the clergy were the Church and that the laity existed only to listen, to obey, and to reach for their wallets. Others pointed out that Rome had never really had a doctrine of the Church, and, when asked for her doctrine of the Church, had always replied with her doctrine of the ministry. She must get used to the idea that the laity are the Church and the hierarchy exist for no other reason than to help them be the Church.

There remains, no doubt, a vast gulf between the Roman and the Protestant concepts of authority, but, in the three ways I have tried to describe, the gulf has appreciably narrowed and brought us at least within hailing distance of one another. Accordingly I want to conclude this lecture by considering briefly three points which we for our part would want to put on the agenda for dialogue.

1. Continuity and Discontinuity

The churches of the Catholic and Orthodox traditions have a deep sense of the continuity of the church, from which we are only just beginning to learn. We have been prepared to speak with pride about our founding fathers and our Congregational inheritance, but we have not drawn any theological conclusions from this about the nature of the Church and its authority. Historical transmission of some sort is inescapable in Christianity, since our faith has its roots in historic facts, with which we can have contact only because they are handed down to us across the centuries. Paul could insist that his apostleship and his gospel came to him direct from Christ and not from human source or through human mediation; but he could also speak of handing on what he himself had received. It will not do for us to say that the whole apostolic tradition is contained in Scripture, so that we need no mediating tradition to put us in contact with the sources of our faith, for we should never have read the Bible if it had not come to us through the living experience of a community continuous with the Church of past generations.

On the other hand, there is in the Bible teaching a strong strain of discontinuity, which seems to me as yet almost wholly unacknowledged in Roman Catholic thought. Saul is anointed king and then deposed. David succeeds him and is given a promise that his dynasty will never fail; yet a little more than four centuries later the Davidic line has been dethroned, never to be restored. There are prophets who belong to professional guilds, and others, like Elisha, who are anointed by a predecessor. But the great prophets are not among them. Amos hotly denies standing in any succession or belonging to any trade union. 'I was no prophet or prophet's son . . . the Lord took me from following the flock.' The prophet wields an authority which he receives direct from God and not through any human succession. John the Baptist warns his contemporaries that physical descent from Abraham will be no advantage in the coming crisis of divine judgement, since God can create sons of Abraham from the desert stones; and Paul echoes his teaching when he says that the true sons of Abraham are not those who can trace their lineage from him in unbroken descent, but those who share his faith. Jesus predicts that God's vineyard will be taken from its present tenants and given to others. Asked by the apostles to rebuke an unlicensed evangelist, he rebukes instead the apostles, and through them all who have supposed that there could be no authority without authorization, and have tried to confine the grace of God within official channels. And finally the Epistle to the Hebrews points out that Jesus, the great High Priest, could not have been a priest at all if he had had to rely on historic succession, since he came from Judah and a priest must be descended from Levi; on the contrary, Jesus stands in the order of Melchizedek, who is notorious for having no genealogy.

I expect you have heard, as I often have heard, the idea of a valid historical succession defended on the grounds that God is not bound by his own rules, but we are. I think it is high time that this particular argument was shown up for the shoddy claptrap that it is. For the question is not whether God makes occasional exceptions in favour of nonconformists. The question is whether there is not ample evidence both in the Bible and in the history of the Church that God regularly and normally honours men's faith and grants them his presence in ways not allowed for by ecclesiastical theory; that he regularly and normally breaks in upon man's complacence and says, 'Behold, I am doing a new thing!'; that he regularly and normally speaks his words of judgement, consolation, guidance, or demand through men who have no authorization other than his own. To say that God has committed himself to working through a historic succession, but has reserved the right of departing from this method in exceptional circumstances is to say that most of the prophets in the Old Testament, and John the Baptist, Jesus, and Paul in the New Testament, are exceptions to a divine rule which finds its full expression in the temple priesthood in the one case and in the Sadducees and Pharisees in the other.

This question has a particular application to our sacraments. Roman Catholics and some Anglicans would like to say that, though invalid, they are effective. They do not wish to deny that these sacraments have been means of grace by which God has done great things for those who are obviously profoundly Christian. What they do want to deny is a great deal harder to define. An effective sacrament, by our definition as well as theirs, is one in which God is present and active. But God cannot be present invalidly. And since it is admitted that these sacraments are a means which God has been using for over four centuries to work his work of grace in the souls of men, it is surely proper to ask whether they need any further validation. It is an immense advance that both Romans and Anglicans are ready to acknowledge as a fact that God has been continuously at work in the life and worship of communions other than their own, but neither has yet faced the implications of this fact. Sooner or later theory must be made to fit the facts, and not facts made to fit the theory.

In this matter of continuity and discontinuity I am far from claiming that all the truth is on one side. This is clearly a case in which each side has much to learn from the other. I suspect that it is one of the many points where both sides are right in what they affirm and wrong in what they deny or ignore.

2. Principalities and Powers

According to Paul (Rom. 13.1–7), all authority belongs to God, and any earthly authority exists by God's decree and operates in God's name. He is prepared to say this even about the pagan state, and describes the Roman magistrate as God's ordained minister for the maintenance of public order. But he also says (Col. 1.16–20) that all forms of authority—thrones, dominions, principalities, or authorities—though created by God and designed to be brought within the rule of Christ, are subject to corruption by sin, and need to be redeemed and reconciled to God through the Cross. The effect of sin on any form of authority is to transform it into a demonic power, which operates in hostility to God. All earthly authority is therefore ambivalent; for while it retains the stamp of God's original intention, and for that reason should be obeyed, it may in fact be a denial of God's intention and contribute to the sum total of human bondage.

The important point for our purpose is that from this analysis Paul does not exempt religious authority. The supreme religious authority for a Jew was the Law of Moses, which Paul declares to be God's law, 'holy, just, and good'. Yet in his own experience sin was capable of taking even this and distorting it to evil purposes. Sin can use the commandment as a subtle temptation and so bring about the very offence it prohibits. 'I should not have had first-hand acquaintance with covetousness, if the law had not said, "You shall not covet."' (Rom. 7.8.) More particularly, it was Paul's enthusiasm for the law and his determination to protect it against the insidious attacks of Jesus and his followers that made him a persecutor of the Church and an open enemy of God. So far from bringing him to God, the law had been a veil over his heart, a means whereby Satan, the god of this world, had blinded the minds of the unbelieving to keep them from seeing the light of the gospel of the glory of Christ (2 Cor. 3.14–4.4). There is no authority given among men which is so high or so holy that it cannot become an instrument of Satan.

What Paul expresses in highly theological, not to say mythological, language is illustrated in simpler terms in the gospel story. Jesus deals leniently and sympathetically with the outcast and untouchable, and reserves his severest strictures for the ecclesiastical authorities, whom he accuses of having locked the book of the knowledge of God and thrown away the key. The testimony of Scripture is amply borne out in the history of the Church. I am at a loss to know whence came the astonishing theory that church officials and leaders are less liable than others to sin and error. I am fully persuaded that when Christ calls men into his service he supports them and furnishes them with the gifts and graces necessary for their task; but I can find no evidence that permanent immunity from the corruption of power is one of those gifts.

At this point I must qualify something I said in the first of these lectures. Among many reasons for confidence that a mutually profitable dialogue is now possible between ourselves and Rome, I drew your attention to passages in the documents of Vatican II which speak of the Church's need for penitence and reformation. I still think these are among the most remarkable and hopeful utterances in the whole corpus of decrees. But there is one note lacking. I find here no clear recognition of the scriptural insight into the corporate nature of evil, the existence of principalities and powers which reach their tentacles into the innermost fabric of our common life, perpetuating themselves not only in individual habit but in social custom and in law, and finding their most durable stronghold in structures of authority. 'While Christ "holy, innocent, undefiled", knew nothing of sin, but came to expiate only the sins of the people, the Church, embracing sinners in her bosom, is at the same time holy and always in need of being purified, and incessantly pursues the path of penance and renewal' (Const. on the Church, par. 8). There is an individualism here which fails to do justice to biblical truth. The sins which put the church in need of penance and renewal are the cumulative debit accounts of her individual members. There is no suggestion that the Church herself might be guilty of corporate sins which could not be laid at the door of any particular person (as we have come to recognize slums and wars as corporate sins in the life of nations). I do not say that the Council Fathers would have denied this truth, but simply that it does not seem to have dawned on their field of vision.

We are, indeed, carried a step nearer to scriptural doctrines in the Decree on Ecumenism. 'Christ summons the Church, as she goes on her pilgrim way, to that continual reformation of which she always has need, insofar as she is an institution of men here on earth' (par. 6). I still thank God for what is here explicitly affirmed, though I am not sure that I know exactly what it means. The need for reformation is said to apply to the Church only in a certain limited sense, but the extent of the limit is obscure. Are we being told that, although the Church has a true life which is hidden with Christ in God, its earthly life as a whole is in constant need of reformation? If so, this would be a thoroughly Pauline doctrine, and I should have to withdraw much of what I have just said. Or are we being told that the earthly Church has a human and fallible side to it which requires reformation, but is also the wielder of a divinely guaranteed authority which does not? The statement of Vatican I, reaffirmed at Vatican II, that certain dogmatic formulations are *ex sese irreformabiles* (by their very nature unalterable) strongly suggests that the second interpretation is the only one which could have been intended by the Council Fathers. But in that case I am justified in thinking that they have shown hardly a hint of the biblical teaching about the ambivalence of *all* authority.

In pastoral psychology it is a commonplace that a man may regret his actions without being truly penitent. He was not at his best, he did not do himself justice, he was not up to his normal standard. The better self sits in judgement on the lower self, the I on the me, the ego on the id; and by this device the better self remains innocent, impenitent, and unforgiven. Repentance comes with the recognition that there is no better self, only the self confronting the judgement and mercy of God. I cannot avoid the feeling that the Church of Rome is still determined to have a better self, a last citadel not exposed either to the assaults of Satan or to the cleansing judgements of God. If this is true, no comment can be more apt than that with which Anselm answered those who asked why God could not forgive without going to the trouble of the Incarnation and the Cross. *Nondum considerasti quanti ponderis sit peccatum.* You have not yet reckoned with the full weight of sin.

We Congregationalists sometimes unreasonably resent the statement that we have a democratic polity. C. S. Lewis used to say that the only Christian reason for believing in democracy was not any nonsense about *vox populi vox Dei*, but the recognition that all men are so sinful that none may safely be trusted with autocratic power. I have long felt that the arguments in favour of episcopacy are impressive. I am held up by a doubt about its effect on bishops. Have we any right to put a man in a position of such appalling exposure? And how many men who have experienced such exposure would claim to have survived it unscathed? I am not offering this as as decisive objection to episcopacy, for I am about to argue that Christianity is a dangerous religion, and that the biggest mistake Christians have ever committed has been to try and make it safe. But I do not think anyone should be an advocate for episcopacy unless he has faced the full implications of Paul's teaching about principalities and powers.

3. *Trembling for the Ark*

There is a familiar Old Testament story about the aged Eli sitting outside the temple at Shiloh, trembling for the ark of God, which his sons had carried into battle. When he heard that the ark was captured and his sons killed, he fell off his chair and broke his neck. His daughter-in-law gave premature birth to a son, whom she saddled with the name Non-glory. But the sequel proved that all this was sheer unbelief. God was well able to look after his own ark, and the Philistines were soon heartily glad to be rid of it.

The message of this story has been taken to heart in some quarters at least in Rome. The Declaration on Religious Liberty, in a sentence I have already quoted, states that 'the truth cannot impose itself except by virtue of its own truth.' There is no need to tremble for the ark of God's truth, or to prop it up with the guarantees of extraneous authority. Truth carries its own credentials, and to supply it with testimonials is tantamount to unbelief.

D

This is the point of the story, recorded more than once in the Gospels, in which Jesus is asked for a sign, that is, for some demonstrative proof of his credentials, some guarantee that his preaching is the word of God. He not only refuses the request, but stigmatizes his interrogators as a wicked and adulterous (i.e. disloyal) generation. If they knew God and loved God as they claimed to know and love him, they would unerringly recognize the word of God when they heard it. The word of God carries its own credentials, and their demand for validation was proof of the insincerity of their own faith.

The same point is made frequently in the Old Testament in connexion with the phenomenon of false prophecy. A man inspired by God must be received and obeyed as God's messenger. But suppose, as not uncommonly happened, two inspired men contradicted one another. How could you tell which was the genuine prophet? The Book of Deuteronomy (18.21–22) offers what seems a piece of common sense: wait and see. If the prophecy comes true, the man is from God. Unfortunately this is not such good advice as it sounds. When Jonah went to Nineveh and said, 'In forty days Nineveh will be in ruins unless you repent', 'wait and see' was precisely the wrong response. Elsewhere Deuteronomy is more helpful. Men must use their own God-given judgement to decide; 'for the Lord your God is testing you to see whether you love the Lord your God with heart and soul' (13.3). In other words, God has deliberately allowed the possibility of false prophecy, the possibility of radical error in religion, because he wanted to provide a test and a training-ground for religious loyalty. However much he may care for accuracy, there is something he cares for more—the trained judgement of men whose loyalty enables them to recognize the word of God. As Jesus said,

'If any man wills to do God's will, he shall know about my teaching, whether it comes from God or whether I have spoken on my own authority.' The word of God is self-authenticating to those who have the moral qualifications to discern it. But God has hedged his revelation about with the possibility of error, because it is precisely in those moral qualifications that his purpose for human life is to be found. His word is 'solid meat for grown men, those who have their faculties exercised by constant use to discriminate between good and evil' (Heb. 5.14).

What the Bible has to say about the authority of God's word is borne out at every point by the history of the Bible in the Church. Those who so tremble for the word of God that they must furnish it with extraneous guarantees of its inerrancy have to reckon with three inescapable facts. The history of textual criticism and the proliferation of variant readings prove that God has made no attempt to provide an infallible text of Scripture. A comparison of the translations made into any one of the hundreds of languages into which the Bible has been translated, or even a comparison of the Latin Vulgate with the Greek and Hebrew, proves that God has in no way protected his word against mistranslation. The most cursory acquaintance with the history of preaching, before or after the Reformation, shows that God has offered no guarantee against misinterpretation. Many a powerful sermon has been preached on a text which proved to be mistranslation of a false reading; and which of us is to say that souls were not saved by them? In the face of such overwhelming accumulation of evidence, how can we evade the conclusion that God is not interested in servile submission to the guarantees of ecclesiastical authority, Catholic or Protestant, but only in the spontaneous love and loyalty which, through all the possibilities of error, can recognize and respond to his truth.

I should like to think that the Council Fathers are in fundamental agreement with what I have been trying to say. There is much in the documents of the Council that encourages that belief, as we shall see in the next lecture, when I deal with the type of Christian character which it is the Church's mission to produce. But this new insight into the self-authenticating nature of truth sits in uneasy juxtaposition with more traditional utterances about the *magisterium* as the necessary guardian and guarantee of revelation.

Further than this I do not profess to see. But I think what I have been pleading for in all three of my points is this. Our concepts of church order and the authority inherent in it must be dictated not simply by a sound doctrine of the Church but by an adequate doctrine of God. We have in Scripture a revelation of the way in which God exercises his authority over man. Apart from rules of procedure, for which we should not expect any biblical precedent, and which in any case ought to be kept under strict control, we ought not to arrogate to any minister an authority incompatible with what we know to be true about God. God is omnipotent; but we must not misunderstand omnipotence as Milton's Satan misunderstood it.

> Farewell happy fields
> Where joy for ever dwells: hail, horrors, hail
> Infernal world, and thou profoundest Hell
> Receive thy new possessor: one who brings
> A mind not to be changed by place or time.
> The mind is its own place, and in itself
> Can make a Heaven of Hell, a Hell of Heaven.
> What matter where, if I be still the same?

Satan regarded omnipotence as an attack on his integrity, and heroically but tragically refused to be coerced into a denial of his self. Tragically, because the true nature of omnipotence is revealed by Jesus to be not unlimited coercion, but the unlimited persuasion of invincible love. When Jesus says to his disciples, 'Whoever would be great among you must be your servant' (Mark 10.43), that could mean that to earn promotion you must undergo an apprenticeship of humility, learn to obey before you can command; or it could, and I think does, mean that in Christ's kingdom no greatness is recognized but the greatness of service. When Jesus says, 'All authority in heaven and on earth has been given to me', this could mean that the humble Nazarene has now been promoted to a status out of all proportion to his lowly beginnings; or it could, and I think does, mean that from that moment on all authority must be interpreted in the light of our knowledge of that earthly figure in whom alone we can see the Father.

4. *The Church's Mission*

ALL Sunday School children know that Nehemiah was a hero. Against a dead weight of Jewish apathy, and in the teeth of determined resistance from the leaders of the neighbouring peoples, he rebuilt the ruined walls of Jerusalem. No Jew could ever forget the picture of his loyal band of followers, building with trowel in one hand and sword in the other, and the trumpeter standing at the ready to sound the alarm. Was not this an answer to prayer, the prayers which had been offered for nearly a hundred and fifty years, ever since the armies of Nebuchadrezzar had destroyed the city?

> Do good to Zion in thy good pleasure;
> Rebuild the walls of Jerusalem.
> Then wilt thou delight in right sacrifice. (Ps. 51.18–19.)

Two and a half centuries later Jesus ben-Sira was to inscribe Nehemiah's name in the roll of honour of his nation's history.

> Nehemiah too has left a lasting memory,
> Who raised our fallen walls,
> Erected gates and bars,
> And rebuilt our ruined homes. (Ecclus. 49.13.)

Nehemiah was certainly a hero. But was he right? Was he right to rebuild a wall which was designed not only to protect but to exclude? Was he right to exclude from the city of God

Samaritans and Ammonites, Ashdodites and Arabs, who until his arrival had mixed freely with the Jews in a single, undivided community? Was he right to put a ban on mixed marriages?

The children who learn about Nehemiah in Sunday School will discover the point of these questions as soon as they grow up and become members of the Church Youth Club. Ought they to restrict the membership to those who are avowedly Christian, and keep up the religious tone, at the risk of losing contact with the young people outside, who have no church connexion? Or should they open the club to all comers and hope that it will not lose its distinctively Christian character? Either choice is dangerous. The only safety seems to be a precarious, knife-edge balance between the two.

Nehemiah no doubt believed that the segregation he advocated was the only way of saving the Jewish religion and the revelation of God that it enshrined from being assimilated to the general religious pattern of Near Eastern syncretism. But he initiated a policy of Jewish particularism which could end only in the ghetto. In New Testament times both the Pharisees and the Qumran covenanters went to even greater lengths in their attempts to answer the question: How can Israel be the holy people of God in a world overrun by paganism? Not content with Nehemiah's wall of separation, the Pharisees surrounded themselves with a massive bulwark of religious regulations, designed to prevent any contact with the contaminations of the sinful world; and for the Qumran community nothing less would suffice than the physical isolation of the Judaean wilderness. A large part of the quarrel that the Pharisees had with Jesus was that he was deliberately breaking down the defences they had been at such pains to erect. In vain did he warn them that to make survival the dominant aim of religion is the certain road to death. 'Whoever would save his life shall lose it.' Even the final destruction of Nehemiah's wall in A.D. 70 by the armies of Titus, which Jesus had constantly predicted, was taken by the Pharisees as a trumpet call to build the walls of their exclusive religious system a little higher and a little stouter than before.

All the while this 'Little Israel' policy was developing, there was no lack of spokesmen on the other side. Seventy-five years before Nehemiah, when Jerusalem still lay in ruins, Zechariah had had a vision of a new Jerusalem without a city wall. 'Jerusalem shall be inhabited as villages without walls, because of the multitude of men and cattle in it. For I will be to her a wall of fire round about, says the Lord.' The Book of Ruth, which we too often treat as a harvest idyll, was a violent protest against a policy which would have deprived Israel of her most famous son; for from the mixed marriage between Boaz and the Moabite Ruth came King David. And the Book of Jonah was intended to be a satire on the narrow, nationalistic Jew, who at the very suggestion that he might help to bring about the penitence and salvation of Nineveh took a one-way ticket on a boat to Spain. Thus Jesus could claim the authority of the Old Testament when he set out to break down the middle wall of partition which Jewish legalism had erected between saint and sinner, between Jew and Gentile.

I have been trying to remind you that our modern debate about the nature of the Church and its mission is at least as old as the Old Testament. They were already asking the questions which we still find ourselves asking today. How can the Church be in the world without being conformed to the world? Which is the Church's primary function, the sanctification of its members or its mission to the pagan world? Should

Christians try to be different, or should they rather avoid anything that would cut them off from the common life of humanity?

There is a sense in which all these questions are a little unreal. Particularism and universalism are not mutually exclusive points of view, Indeed, the one can hardly exist without the other. There is no point in talking about a world-wide mission unless you are so different from the rest of mankind that you have something to offer them. Nehemiah was right to this extent, that Israel could hardly be a light to the Gentiles if she failed to keep her lamp topped up with oil. He was wrong if he imagined that, by putting Israel's lamp under a flour-bin to protect it from the blasts of paganism, he was doing the work of God.

The way we look at this question is profoundly affected by what we conceive to be God's ultimate purpose for mankind. There are two schools of thought, both able to appeal to biblical, and even dominical, authority. The one which has had the greatest popularity in the history of the Church I call the vacancy theory. According to this theory the whole elaborate scheme of creation is only a backdrop to a human drama, the purpose of which is to enable God to make up the number of his elect. He has a certain number of places to fill. Last summer, in an examination I was marking, candidates were asked to comment on the verse in the Fourth Gospel which describes Peter's remarkable catch of fish. The number 153, said one candidate, is the number of those who will be gathered up at the last day. Others, with slightly greater optimism, have settled for 144,000, whether literally or symbolically. It is characteristic of this view that the elect are brands plucked from the burning. God is interested only in individual souls, not in the products of their hands or brains, nor in the hopes, aspirations, and achievements which constitute their secular existence. Provided he may fill his heavenly vacancies, the whole cosmic process, including the triumphs of the human genius and spirit, may ultimately be cast as rubbish to the void. The alternative view, which Tennyson called 'the larger hope', is that God has a purpose not only for individual souls, but for the whole creation with which men's lives are so indissolubly linked.

The history of missions forbids us to suppose that missionary zeal is necessarily allied to the larger hope. The doctrine of election and the vivid belief in fiery judgement which has been its normal corollary have often supplied a greater incentive and sense of urgency to missionary enthusiasm than the rival theory. But it clearly makes a world of difference to the shape of the Church's mission whether you believe God to be interested in man's intellectual and cultural achievements and in his political and social progress, or only in his soul. Those who think in terms of individual salvation will be likely to agree with Nehemiah that the Church's first task is to maintain its own sanctity, so that converts may be brought from the dangers of worldly corruption into the security of the holy community. Those who believe that God has a wider purpose are more likely to lower the barriers between the Church and the world.

I hope that this long introduction may help you to appreciate the quite extraordinary skill and insight with which the Council Fathers have dealt with this notoriously difficult subject in the four documents which are concerned with the church's mission—the two Decrees on the Apostolate of the Laity and on the Church's Missionary Activity, the Declaration on the Relationship of the Church to Non-Christian Religions, and the Pastoral Constitution on the Church in the Modern

World. The first of these documents has a paragraph on the goals of mission which I think is worth quoting in full.

Christ's redemptive work, while of itself directed toward the salvation of men, involves also the renewal of the whole temporal order. Hence the mission of the Church is not only to bring to men the message and grace of Christ, but also to penetrate and perfect the temporal sphere with the spirit of the gospel. In fulfilling this mission of the Church, the laity, therefore, exercise their apostolate both in the Church and in the world, in both the spiritual and the temporal orders. These realms, although distinct, are so connected in the one plan of God that He Himself intends in Christ to appropriate the whole universe into a new creation, initially here on earth, fully on the last day. In both orders, the layman, being simultaneously a believer and a citizen, should be constantly led by the same Christian conscience (par. 5).

I take this to mean that the Church has the task of bringing men out of the world into a spiritual community in which they may be trained in the Christian life, furnished with Christian gifts and graces, and made fit to be partakers in the inheritance of the saints in light. But, since the kingdom of heaven is anticipated here on earth in Christ's claim to be lord over all creation, the very qualities which fit a man for holiness in heaven are also those which equip him to go out into the world as the agent of Christ's transforming and renewing power. There is therefore no clash between the particularist and the universalist aims of the Church. It cannot be the saved community unless it is at the same time the saving community; and it is the saving community, not because those already in the ark reach out rescuing hands to shipwrecked mariners drowning in the ocean of life, but because they are shock-troops, ready to land on every part of the secular order and to take possession of it in the name of Christ.

Let us then examine the Council documents in greater detail to see how this double purpose is conceived, taking each part of it in turn.

1. *Christian Maturity*

The first function of the Church then is to educate men to the full stature of Christian manhood. In the older manuals of pastoral theology this aim would certainly have been described in terms of holiness of life, nurture in the sacraments, and submission to the authority of the Church. I do not mean to imply that any of these elements is wholly neglected today, but the emphasis has shifted, as may be seen from this somewhat startling passage from the Decree on the Ministry and Life of Priests. 'Therefore, as educators in the faith, priests must see to it, either by themselves or through others, that the faithful are led individually in the Holy Spirit to a development of their own vocation as required by the gospel, to a sincere and active charity, and to that freedom with which Christ has made us free. Ceremonies however beautiful, or associations however flourishing, will be of little value if they are not directed toward educating men in the attainment of Christian maturity' (par. 6). The succeeding paragraph explains that maturity is attained only through the fullest discharge of a man's responsibility in society.

This last point is put clearly, albeit somewhat fulsomely, in the Decree on Education.

Since every man of whatever race, condition, and age is endowed with the dignity of a person, he has an inalienable right to an education corresponding to his proper destiny and suited to his native talents, his sex, his cultural background, and his ancestral heritage. At the same time, this education should pave the way to brotherly association with other peoples, so that genuine unity and peace on earth may be promoted. For a true education aims at the formation of the human person with respect to his ultimate goal, and simultaneously with respect to the good of those societies of which, as a man, he is a member, and in whose responsibilities, as an adult, he will share. As a consequence, with the help of advances in psychology and in the art and science of teaching, children and young people should be assisted in the harmonious development of their physical, moral, and intellectual endowments. Surmounting hardships with a gallant and steady heart, they should be helped to acquire gradually a more mature sense of responsibility toward ennobling their own lives through constant effort, and toward pursuing authentic freedom (par. 1).

Maturity has thus two components: a responsible freedom, enabling a man to see for himself 'what is required and what is God's will in the great and small events of life'; and the development of those skills and talents which each man must discover in himself and contribute to the effective life of the Church both in its own community and in its work in the world. In the Decree on the Apostolate of the Laity this double concept of maturity is related to two biblical ideas which have hitherto been considered a feature of Protestantism, the priesthood of all believers and the charismatic gifts of the Spirit. 'They are consecrated into a royal priesthood and a holy people (cf. 1 Pet. 2.4–10) in order that they may offer spiritual sacrifices through everything they do, and may witness to Christ throughout the world. . . . For the exercise of this apostolate, the Holy Spirit who sanctifies the People of God through the ministry and the sacraments gives to the faithful special gifts as well (cf. 1 Cor. 12.7), "allotting to everyone according as he will" (1 Cor. 12.11). . . . From the reception of these charisms or gifts, including those which are less dramatic, there arise for each believer the right and duty to use them in the Church and in the world for the good of mankind and for the upbuilding of the Church' (par. 3).

In the teaching of Luther the priesthood of all believers seems to have had both a negative and a positive aspect. Negatively it was the claim that all believers have the right of free access to God without the intervention of hierarchical authority, and in this sense it could equally well have been called the non-priesthood of any believers. Positively it was a declaration of the mutual dependence of all Christians on one another for the maintenance of a truly evangelical piety. 'I need my brother's voice as the human instrument by which God assures me of his grace. God appoints my neighbour to be his representative. Through the voice of the brother, the preaching man, the power of the keys is exercised on my behalf, and I am assured of absolution and forgiveness.' (J. S. Whale, *The Protestant Tradition*, p. 110). In later and debased forms of Protestantism the priesthood of all believers tended to become a quite unscriptural egalitarianism, a belief that all Christians are equally endowed and equally entitled to perform all functions within the Church. It is an impressive and sobering thought that the Church of Rome should not only find it possible to adopt as her own the battle-cry once raised in revolt against her, but should also fill it with new meaning by a more meticulous exegesis of Scripture. The second chapter of 1 Peter is correctly taken to mean that the priestly duties of the Christian community include both the offering of its whole life as a spiritual sacrifice within the Church and the publishing of the mighty powers of God to the outside world; and both functions are directly related to Paul's teaching about spiritual gifts.

Some Protestants have been accustomed to use the Pauline

doctrine of spiritual gifts as an answer to Roman claims about the hierarchical ministry. If all ministries in the church are the gift of the Spirit who 'breathes where he wills', then no system of historic transmission can either guarantee or limit the activity of the Spirit. I think most of us now recognize that this argument involves a false antithesis. It is possible, as our own practice of ordination shows, for a man who has received a particular gift of the Spirit to be appointed to an office in which that gift may be exercised to the full, without such an appointment being an attempt to control the Spirit. Rome has admittedly been hesitant about applying the idea of charismatic gifts to the priesthood, but nothing could be more Congregational than the way in which she is now applying it to the laity. Whatever may be said about the special position of the ordained ministry, it is clearly stated that every church member has his own personal ministry, which he must exercise both in the Church and in the world. And it is along these lines that we are invited to take a fresh look at the priesthood of all believers. If all Christians have a share in the priestly character of the Church, it is not because all are equally and identically endowed, so that A must do for B and C exactly what B does for C and A. It is because all are differently endowed, and the combined gifts of all are needed if the Church is either to offer her life in fitting sacrifice to God or adequately to discharge her mission to the world. The Church, in fact, is not a pod full of peas. It is an organism in which each part has a highly diversified function.

Although this doctrine of the church is as old as Paul, it is almost as new to Protestants as it is to Catholics. Catholics have been so busy asserting the hierarchical structure of the church, and Protestants so busy denying it, that neither have had much time or energy to spare to do justice to the idea of the Church as a team of thoroughly variegated talent. The old assumption of Rome was that whatever a layman could do, a deacon could do, and more besides; whatever a deacon could do, a priest could do, and more; whatever a priest could do, a bishop could do, and more; and whatever a bishop could do, the Pope could do, and more. Now they are coming to realize that the actual differences in the Church are not hierarchical, but functional. There are tasks in the world which the layman can perform, from which any ordained minister is debarred by the very fact of his ordination. The exalted status of the Pope makes it impossible for him to be to the ordinary layman what the parish priest can be. And they have now restored the diaconate as a permanent lifelong office, recognizing that its functions are different from those of the priesthood. As Paul says, there are varieties of gifts; and the least honourable is not necessarily the least important.

One of the commonest criticisms made by Congregationalists about their own form of churchmanship is that it provides far too little training in the disciplines of the religious life; and we are often asked whether we could not take a leaf out of the book of those who have long experience in the holding of retreats. I once made this point to a Roman Catholic friend, who replied: 'The only trouble with a retreat is that it so easily becomes a rout.' This was more than a piece of witty repartee. There is something of the Nehemiah mentality in the picture of the Church as a refuge from the storms of life, which is not easily squared with the more robust spirit of the New Testament. According to the teaching of Vatican II the Church would be better compared to a powerhouse, in which Christians are charged with a new access of energy for their life in the world. Even the chapter of the Dogmatic Constitution on the

Church which deals with the religious orders emphasizes the necessity of monastic involvement in the life of the secular world. 'Let no one think that by their consecration religious have become strangers to their fellow men or useless citizens of this earthly city. For even though in some instances religious do not directly mingle with their contemporaries, yet in a more profound sense these same religious are united with them in the heart of Christ and co-operate with them spiritually. In this way the work of building up the earthly city can always have its foundation in the Lord and can tend toward Him. Otherwise, those who build this city will perhaps have laboured in vain' (par. 46).

This description of the church as a training ground in Christian maturity seems to me to be one point at which we might expect very general agreement among all Christians, though there might be some differences of opinion about the degree of worldly involvement to which the church was thus committed. But supposing we made this the starting point for further dialogue, what effect would it have upon our traditional conceptions of church order? I have already suggested that it is bound to modify the hierarchical assumption of Rome. But what of ourselves? Can we really maintain that the local church as it existed in the static society of the seventeenth century is still, in the vastly changed conditions of the twentieth century, an adequate training ground for the sort of responsible churchmanship envisaged by the Council Fathers? Do we in our current practice leave such training to the initiative and authority of the local congregation? Has the time perhaps come for us to reconsider what we mean by 'local', now that the very idea of locality has been transformed by modern communications, and a man in London can make a 'local' telephone call to his neighbour in Aberdeen? Nobody doubts, the Church of Rome least of all, that the local church in some sense must continue to be the focus of all Christian activity. It is noteworthy, however, that the documents of Vatican II sometimes speak of those particular churches which are to embody the full character of the one universal Church, and by this they mean not the parish but the diocese. Has the time come when we should be experimenting with a local unit much larger than a single congregation and much smaller than the present Roman or Anglican diocese, led by a team of ministers trained in a variety of ministerial skills? If so, then certainly it is only by a union of churches that we could achieve a proper concentration of talent which would make such a church at the same time more truly episcopal and more truly congregational than anything that exists today.

2. *The Dominion of Christ*

Christian maturity is not, however, to be regarded as an end in itself, nor even as an attainable end, apart from the Church's mission to the world. There is no question of the Christian athlete reaching full spiritual fitness before he has to enter the arena of the world mission. On the contrary, maturity is reached only by means of a responsible exercise of one's gifts in the life of the earthly city. Perfection of individual character is a by-product of the Church's mission to bring the whole world within the sovereignty of Christ. We must turn now to see how this theme is handled in the Pastoral Constitution on the Church in the Modern World.

The Church's concern, we are told, is not just with man's religious life but with all his needs, desires, aspirations, and achievements, however much these may have been tainted by sin. Man is made in the image of God, and nothing that can be considered truly human can be alien to the interest of God. If man is to be saved, he must be saved in his integrity, and not by the dismemberment of his life into sacred and secular. In particular, man is not an individual but a person. An individual can be treated as an isolated unit, but a person is the centre of a complex network of relationships. Any doctrine of salvation which deracinates man from his social setting is an infringement of the true dignity of man. This means, amongst other things, that the Church must furnish for the guidance of its members something more than an individualistic ethic. It means too that the Church must at all times be concerned with social justice. To believe in the Incarnation is to believe in human solidarity and in the value of all legitimate human activity in the eyes of God.

All this could have been said in such a way as to carry us straight back to the Middle Ages, when the church claimed direct authority over the whole of life. But it is not the purpose of this document to turn back the clock. It contains an explicit declaration of the autonomy of the secular. The sciences rightly operate by their own laws and must not have their findings dictated to them by any other authority, political or ecclesiastical. The arts give rise to their own aesthetic standards and are only degraded if they are made to act as handmaids to morality. Men's political and economic activities have similarly their own proper norms. If Theology is ever again to be Queen of the Sciences, she must agree to be a constitutional monarch and not a despot.

What then can be meant by bringing these autonomous fields of human effort within the sovereignty of Christ? The answer is that all human endeavour is in constant danger of being corrupted by the sins of pride and greed, of being dehumanized, of losing its independence in some form of tyranny or bondage. So far from depriving man's secular activities of their proper autonomy, the Christian doctrine of redemption is the one means by which that autonomy can be preserved. The church's mission to the world is not to dominate but to liberate. Family life, science, art, and culture, politics and economics—all contribute to the fullness of man's world and all are the field of God's redemptive activity.

It is remarkable enough that the Church of Rome should have awakened from her haunted sleep to so magnificent a vision as this. But there is more to come. What she has said about man's secular aspirations and achievements, she is prepared to say also about those religions which she once denounced as pagan superstition.

The Catholic Church rejects nothing which is true and holy in these religions. She looks with sincere respect upon those ways of conduct and of life, those rules and teachings which, though differing in many particulars from what she holds and sets forth, nevertheless often reflect a ray of that Truth which enlightens all men. . . . The Church therefore has this exhortation for her sons: prudently and lovingly, through dialogue and collaboration with the followers of other religions, and in witness of Christian faith and life, acknowledge, preserve, and promote the spiritual and moral goods found among these men, as well as the values in their society and culture. (Decl. on the Church's Relation to Non-Chr. Religions, par. 2).

The same atmosphere pervades the Decree on Missions. The object of missionary activity is to bring Christ and his healing power to the nations of the world; but this is not to be carried out simply by converting men to Christianity and transferring them from their former religion and culture to an alien setting.

'Whatever truth and grace are to be found among the nations, as a sort of secret presence of God, this activity frees from all taint of evil and restores to Christ its maker. . . . And so, whatever good is found to be sown in the hearts and minds of men, or in the rites and cultures peculiar to various peoples, is not lost' (par. 9). Christ has been given the nations as his inheritance. 'From the customs and traditions of their people, from their wisdom and their learning, from their arts and sciences, these churches borrow all those things which can contribute to the glory of their Creator, the revelation of the Saviour's grace, or the proper arrangement of Christian life' (par. 22). The document freely recognizes the immensity of the undertaking it proposes. It calls for the establishment of original and creative theological investigation in each major socio-cultural area, so that the dialogue between the Church and the indigenous religion and culture may be carried on. This will involve not only a searching critique of the non-Christian religion, but a fresh scrutiny of the Christian tradition, so that 'faith can seek for understanding in the philosophy and wisdom of thsee peoples.' And all this must be done in such a way that 'every appearance of syncretism and of false particularism can be excluded, and Christian life can be accommodated to the genius and disposition of each culture.' (ibid.)

This is, of course, just where we came in. For the problem of relating our faith to an alien culture without falling into either a syncretism which would obliterate its distinctive character or a particularism which would cut us off from our neighbours is precisely the problem of Nehemiah. The Vatican Council has firmly repudiated Nehemiah's solution: the walls are down. No doubt from time to time we shall hear the Curial trumpet sounding the alarm. But the Church of Rome has now officially become the pilgrim church, with only a waning interest in building the walls of an earthly Jerusalem, because her eyes are fixed on the better city where the gates are perpetually open to the north, south, east, and west. 'I saw no temple in the city, for its temple was the Lord God Omnipotent and the Lamb. It had no need of sun or moon to shine on it; for the glory of God gave it light, and its lamp was the Lamb. The nations shall walk by its light, and the kings of the earth shall bring into it their treasures. Its gates shall never be shut by day —and there shall be no night there. They will bring into it the treasures and wealth of the nations' (Rev. 21.22–26).

We began where the Vatican Council began, with an idea of dialogue which would enable the divided churches to begin to talk to one another again, hesitantly perhaps, and with a deep awareness of the differences outstanding between them. We have ended where the Council ended, and where the New Testament itself ends, with a vision of vastly enlarged possibility, before which our differences shrink into a proper proportion.

There is a story of a motorist who stopped and asked an Irish farmer the way to Dublin, and received the reply, 'If I was going to Dublin, sure and I wouldn't start from here.' There is a humdrum sense in which we have no choice but to start from where we are. But perhaps these words were spoken altogether for our sakes, on whom the ends of the ages have come. For if in our ecumenical dialogue we start from where we are, still behind the walls of our separate cities, we shall find, like the two women shouting across the street, that we cannot agree while we are arguing from different premises. But if we start, not from where we are, but from where we all know that we ought to be, recognizing that we are pilgrims who share a common road because we are travelling to a common destination, then perhaps, sooner than any of us has yet dared to expect, we may see the Holy City, not waiting for us at the journey's end, but coming down out of heaven from our God, and discover that there is more room in it than we had been given to suppose.